Newcastle
City Council

Newcastle Libraries and Information Service

☎ **0845 002 0336**

Due for return	Due for return	Due for return

Please return this item to any of Newcastle's Libraries by the last
date shown above. If not requested by another customer the loan
can be renewed, you can do this by phone, post or in person.
Charges may be made for late returns.

THE PAINTED QUILT

LINDA & LAURA KEMSHALL

David and Charles

A DAVID & CHARLES BOOK
Copyright © David & Charles Limited 2007

David & Charles is an F+W Publications Inc. company
4700 East Galbraith Road
Cincinnati, OH 45236

First published in the UK in 2007
Reprinted 2008 twice

Text and project designs copyright © Linda & Laura Kemshall 2007
Photography copyright © David & Charles 2007

ISBN-13: 978-0-7153-2449-3 hardback
ISBN-10: 0-7153-2449-7 hardback

ISBN-13: 978-0-7153-2450-9 paperback
ISBN-10: 0-7153-2450-0 paperback

Printed in China by Shenzhen Donnelley Printing Co., Ltd.
for David & Charles
Brunel House   Newton Abbot   Devon

Commissioning Editor Vivienne Wells
Senior Editor Jennifer Fox-Proverbs
Head of Design Prudence Rogers
Production Controller Ros Napper
Project Editor Cathy Joseph
Photographer Karl Adamson

Visit our website at www.davidandcharles.co.uk

David & Charles books are available from all good bookshops; alternatively you can contact our Orderline on
0870 9908222 or write to us at FREEPOST EX2 110, D&C Direct, Newton Abbot, TQ12 4ZZ (no stamp required
UK only); US customers call 800-289-0963 and Canadian customers call 800-840-5220.

Contents

Introduction

What do we mean by a painted quilt? Laura and I use the term in the broadest possible sense to describe any of our quilts that involve the application of paint, print, pastel, dye, image transfer, pen drawing and painted fusible web. Almost any technique you could imagine using to create a painted quilt is very simple when you consider it in isolation. It is using these simple techniques together in appropriate combinations that we believe produces complex and fascinating surfaces.

Previous page: *Dreamtime* by Linda. 97 x 100cm (38 x 39.5in).

Usually we add colour to cloth before it becomes a quilt but, almost always, once the quilt is made and to all intents and purposes appears complete, we add more. Most people might think that is a strange, if not to say reckless, practice. Their concern is understandable as we will already have invested many hours in the making of the quilt and then we, as they see it, take a chance of ruining all the hard work. It is important to understand, though, that colour added when the quilt is quilted isn't some arbitrary or last minute decision. It isn't something we do to redeem a boring colour scheme or add a bit of excitement. It would always have been part of the plan.

Although we may appear to work intuitively on the cloth, this intuition is based on years of drawing, photographing and designing. The colour combinations and the composition of the quilt will have been decided in a sketchbook somewhere, even if that drawing or painting was made a long time before the quilt was created. Sketchbooks are an important aspect of our lives and we revisit old books all the time for inspiration. Even if there appears to be little in the way of finished design work, we have a vision in our mind's eye of the overall proportions of the quilt, the relative size and scale of the elements involved and will have allowed space for the contribution the final painting or printing will make.

You might ask why we make quilts if painting is such a passion. Why don't we just make paintings and forget about quilts altogether? The answer is that colour applied to a quilted surface will produce completely different results to those same techniques used on a single layer of cloth, canvas or paper. Working on to a quilted surface is quite unlike working on to a flat one. The quilted surface is the most important element of our work and there has to be lots of quilting to make it turn out as we want it to. Stitch is quite simply what makes each

Linda's quilt, *Boom Boom Blues*, was made using cotton and woollen fabrics with Markal Paintstik stencilling, colour discharge, machine quilting and hand seeding and beading. 131 x 128cm (51.5 x 50in).

quilt complete. Quilting provides fascinating visual and tactile texture and has an affect on every textile decoration technique we use. There is something elemental about the handling of cloth. Throughout our lives we are in constant contact with fabric. The physical act of holding and stitching fabric is something we both take for granted as a natural daily occurrence, something basic that neither of us could possibly imagine existing without.

"Although we may appear to work intuitively on the cloth, this intuition is based on years of drawing, photographing and designing."

Boom Boom Blues, detail showing machine quilting, hand-stitched seeding and pastel stencilling.

Boom Boom Blues, detail showing pastel stencilling on woollen fabric.

Linda's quilt, *The Fifth Day*, is a wholecloth quilt
painted with fabric paints (see pages 94–95).
36 x 188cm (14 x 74in).

In writing this book we aim to show how
we approach the design process and what
influences our choice of materials and
techniques when we make our quilts. We
describe the characteristics and suitability
of the fabrics and the textile decoration
products that we use. There are so many
products available to anyone working
with textiles these days that it can be
quite bewildering to visit a craft store and
be confronted with shelves heaving with
bottles, boxes and jars. We prefer to keep it
simple, although we do voraciously acquire
every product as it becomes available,
just in case it really is the best new thing!
Our work is produced using a very limited
number of basic items. We describe the
techniques and processes that we use most
often and show lots of examples.

A successful quilt doesn't just rely
on practical or technical skills – ideas are
equally important. This is especially true
for anyone who wants to create their own
unique designs and develop a personal
quilting style. We explain what makes a
good source of inspiration for design and
show the methods we use to record and
develop our ideas into our sketchbooks.

Finally, we demonstrate how we
combine all the techniques we have
discussed in the book when we are making
our own quilts. It's not enough to know
a lot of different techniques or to have a
huge horde of products. The important
thing is to use them thoughtfully and in a
way that is appropriate to the materials, the
inspiration and the desired visual effect. It
is also important to know when a design
is complete; when in fact it is time to stop.
My daughter, Laura, and I work side by side
in the same building and approach the
creative process of designing and making
a quilt in very similar ways. However, our
finished pieces are often quite different.
It is good to know that a tried and tested
formula can still allow one's personality and
individuality to be evident.

"Ideas are just as important

as practical skills."

This detail from Laura's quilt *Morning and Evening*
features an ink-jet print on dyed fabric, with detail
added with fabric paint. 36 x 188cm (14 x 74in).

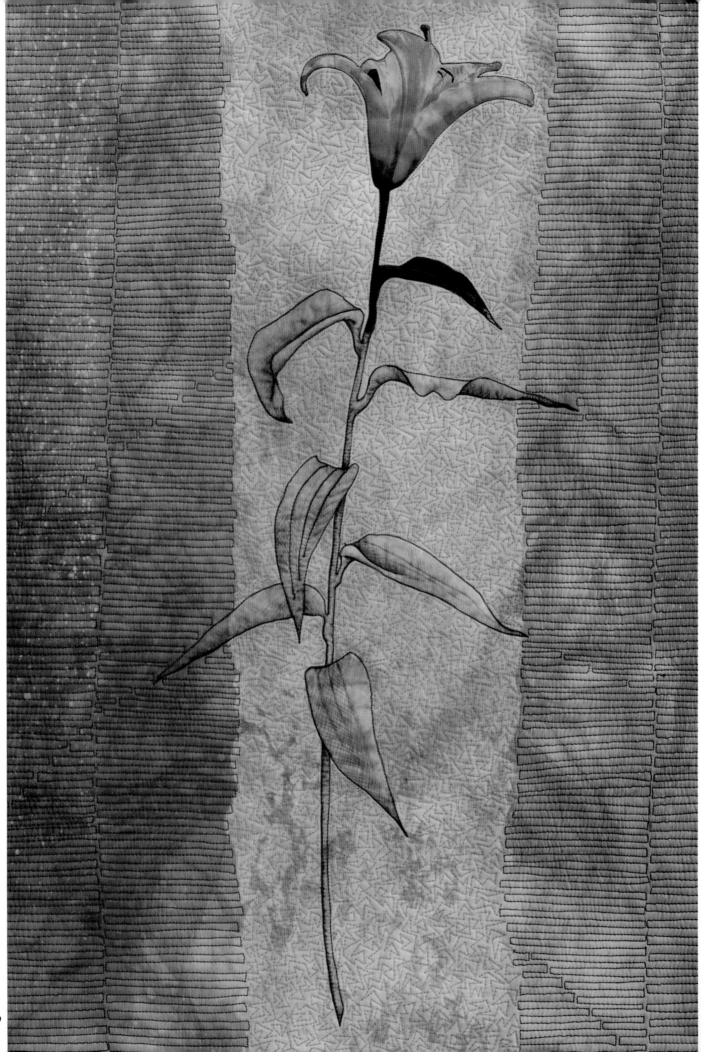

Read through the book and take from it what you will. Not everything that we talk about will be new to every reader but we hope to illustrate how we use some simple techniques in our own work, to show where the inspiration for a quilt or series of work originates and, in particular, how we use several techniques in combination for enhanced effect. We believe that there are many destinations and, indeed, many ways to arrive at the same destination. This book tells of the path we follow, how it works for us and how it might help you to find your own style and approach to designing and making quilts.

We don't pretend our way is the only way. Your path may take you down many fascinating diversions from the main route. You might even find yourself taking a completely unpredicted detour never to return to the original road! What matters isn't where you end up or how you got there, but that you started out in the first place. Take the first steps of your journey with us, learn from our experience, even from our mistakes, and then break free to find your own direction and your own destination.

If you are an avid quiltmaker, you will probably already own some of the basic materials and media that we recommend. You may also own some products that were acquired at a quilt show or quilt class and never used since. Throughout the book we will explain the specific characteristics and applications of a range of products and processes so that those spur of the moment purchases can at last earn their keep!

In Chapter 3 we describe the types of fabrics we use and provide a chart showing which products and processes are suitable for each. Chapter 3 also includes recipes for the basic dyes, pastes and auxiliary solutions. We recommend that you test products and techniques that are new to you and make small samples to gain experience and confidence before planning a more resolved piece of work. Many of the techniques we describe will be equally successful with similar products from different manufacturers. For instance, if we use fabric paint it probably doesn't matter which brand it is, but each paint is likely

Blue Lily **by Laura features an ink-jet transfer using heat transfer paper. A pale, vertical band was bleached through the centre and, finally, details of leaves and stem were drawn with pen. 51cm x 76cm (202 x 30in).**

to be slightly different, thicker, thinner etc. This is another reason to make samples. Remember, whatever you are using, always read the manufacturers' guidelines for specific usage as these override any generic instructions we provide.

The most important thing to bear in mind as you read this book is that you don't have to follow any instructions slavishly. Although, in Chapter 9, we explain how some of our quilts come to be what they are, the information and examples we provide are there to encourage you to find your own inspiration and to follow your own creative path.

"This book tells of the path we follow, how it works for us and how it might help you to find your own style and approach."

Linda's quilt, *Make Your Mark*, a detail of which is shown here, includes simple piecing, appliqué and printing with compressed sponge shapes. 117cm x 137cm (46 x 54in).

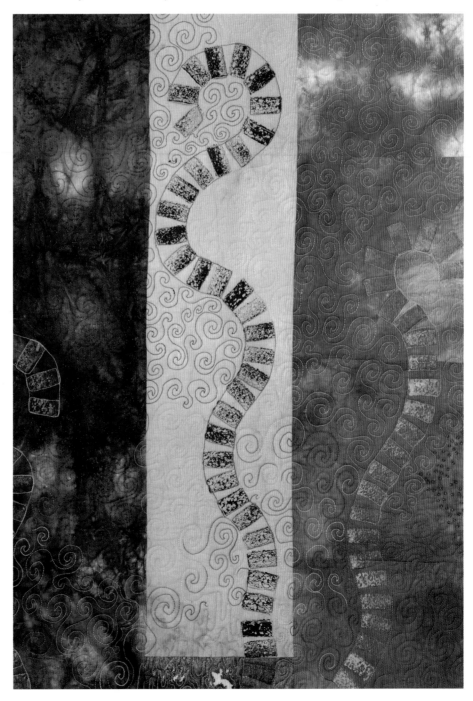

Inspired to Design

We are often asked why we work out ideas on paper first before launching into fabric and thread. Potentially expensive disasters can be avoided by auditioning colour and composition in a sketchbook before acquiring fabrics. If you can achieve a design that is pleasing and attractive on the page, it is almost guaranteed to be equally successful as a quilt. Even more important, playing with design ideas using paper and paint allows for the unexpected to happen. Happy accidents and a little serendipity can produce the most original designs of all. In this chapter we discuss some simple but effective art techniques that will enable you to translate your ideas and create visually exciting sketchbook pages.

Elements of Design

What are we looking for in a source of inspiration? It helps focus the mind to consider the characteristics we should be aware of. The elements of design are the same for all of the visual arts: colour, line, shape, texture and form are the building blocks with which designs are created. Not all these elements are involved in every project, or, if they are, they are not always of equal importance. Sometimes one element will dominate with the remaining ones playing a minor role. Some quilters hesitate to call themselves designers but even the simplest creative choices will involve some of the elements of design.

Previous page: sketchbook and samples by Linda.

Colour

This is often the most significant feature for anyone working with fabrics. It is the element that catches our eye and draws us across a crowded exhibition floor to look more closely at a fantastic quilt. The basic materials we use are often already coloured or we add colour to them as we work. There are recognized rules of colour theory but, despite these, colour is a very personal choice. How boring it would be if we all liked the same things! In this book we stress the value of working from a source of inspiration. If the source is something you find interesting or beautiful and if the colours of it attract you, it will almost certainly provide everything you need to create a successful colour scheme in a quilt.

Images to inspire colour.

Line

A line is defined as a narrow mark connecting two points. We see lines within the landscape in the form of roads, rivers, fences, hedgerows, the edge of the seashore and the distant horizon. Lines in architecture are often horizontal or vertical because of the building materials involved and the methods of construction. With the exception of domes and arches, curves in architecture are usually decorative rather than structural. Lines are also often in the detail of objects: markings on a petal, cracks in peeling paint, rings in wood and veins on an insect wing. Lines within a design can be continuous or broken, narrow or broad, straight, angular or curved. Line is introduced into the design equation as soon as a quilting pattern begins to evolve, but it might also present itself as a striped fabric, a narrow column of appliquéd shapes or a striking colour of binding.

"Becoming aware of the part each element of design plays in a quilt is important for anyone wishing to create their own original work."

Images to inspire line.

TIP Noticing which quilts catch your attention at a show and spending a little time analysing why they appeal is an easy and enjoyable way to develop powers of observation and evaluation. You can find out a lot about yourself and your likes and dislikes this way.

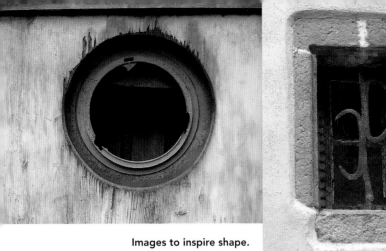

Images to inspire shape.

Shape

This is the area created when a line, or several lines, meet to enclose space. The objects we might involve in a design have a definite shape, for instance a leaf, a bird, a circle or a square, but the area surrounding the object has shape too. We also have to consider the overall shape of the item we are designing and the relationship it has to the shape of the space it will occupy.

Texture

When we talk about texture, we are usually referring to tactile texture, i.e. the quality of the surface determined by touch. This describes whether something is soft, like fur, shiny, like glass, or rough, like rock. Small-scale patterns and variations of colour can also produce something called visual texture, which is completely independent of how the object would feel to the touch. Nature is rarely a single solid colour; more often it involves visual texture because of subtle colour variations. Think of the effect of delicate, mottled patterns of lichen on a rock or the patterns on a chicken's feather. Quilts are a tactile medium, comforting to hold and a pleasure to touch. They also provide visual texture because of their patterns of colour and shape.

Images to inspire texture

Form

In the world of quiltmaking, form is often seen as the least significant element of design because quilts are usually flat. Shape and form are often referred to at the same time. The easiest way to describe the difference between the two is to say that form is three-dimensional, like a cube, and shape is two-dimensional, like a square. Shape has height and width, form has height, width and also depth. 3-D objects include regular geometric forms like cylinders, domes and spheres, all of which might feature in architecture, and organic or irregular forms like the rocks, animals, trees and plants of the natural world. Some 3-D forms, such as a boulder, have a heavy, solid mass, others are open and airy like a bouquet of flowers. Form can completely enclose space, as in the case of a box or hollow sphere, or only partially enclose it as a shallow bowl does. All 3-D objects have volume that occupies 3-D space. Form is obviously an important element for anyone designing quilted garments, cushions, or objects such as boxes when it is vital to consider how the design relates to the surfaces and planes of the object as a whole.

Creating the illusion of form

Of course, it isn't necessary to always be so literally 3-D. Sometimes we design using a conventional quilt format but we might want to create the visual illusion of depth in the design – to make a 2-D surface, or certain areas of the surface, appear 3-D. In design terms, it is perfectly possible to create the impression of depth on a flat plane. By involving a consistent direction of a light source in a composition, the brain interprets the image in the same way it sees objects in the real world. Traditionally, quilters have used illusion in designs such as 'tumbling blocks' where the placement of light, medium and dark colour values produces a convincingly solid looking cube.

Think also of the way a painter uses perspective to make us imagine we are seeing a landscape or the interior of a room. Intellectually we understand that we are only seeing paint marks on a piece of flat canvas but because the lines of the design converge at one or more points on the horizon, the scene appears realistic. In any design, pictorial or abstract, placing large shapes near the bottom of the composition suggests that they are closer to us than any smaller shapes placed nearer the top.

Perspective

In the real world, objects in the distance appear smaller than those close to us even though we may know them to be exactly the same size. Shapes drawn between two converging lines of perspective appear to become gradually smaller. Imagine standing at one end of an avenue of trees. The trees are all more or less the same height but those at the far end of the avenue seem to be tiny compared to the ones close by.

Understanding and using perspective is an effective device for the quiltmaker who can use gradation of size to create movement and direction in a design. The placement of colour or of different colour values in a design can do much the same thing. Some colours appear to advance from the quilt surface, others to recede, just as they do in the landscape. Think how distant mountains often look pale blue or purple while the closer ground is much brighter and more colourful. It is often the brighter and warmer colours that seem to be closer to us, but even these characteristics are relative to the colours that are placed adjacent.

Images to inspire form.

Where to Look for Inspiration

Inspiration can be found just about anywhere, even in the most everyday situations, you just have to see it. You may be able to work from an actual object but sometimes that's not practical. Not many artists would attempt to paint a landscape from memory alone; they would prefer to rely on sketches or photographs taken at the site. It is the same for quiltmakers, too.

Sketchbook page showing photographs.

Working from photographs

Books and magazines can provide exciting images but are never as good as the photographs you take yourself. Copyright issues aside, with a magazine picture you are seeing any subject through the eyes of the professional photographer, not as you yourself would have experienced the scene. Unfortunately, the kind of holiday snaps most people take often don't involve the depth of detail that is needed to develop a successful design. Indeed, a single photo is rarely enough. To fully understand the subject, it is probably necessary to photograph it from several different angles and also to record any specific details that might be useful. Training yourself to be critical about what the camera lens captures is a valuable part of the design process. There are several basic things to consider. Referring to the list of elements of design is a reminder of what you are looking to record and a good place to start.

Light and colour

First consider colour. What is the time of day and what are the weather conditions? The amount and quality of light is what influences the colours we perceive. Light falling on any subject can make it look very different at various times of the day or from season to season.

There is a woodland view that we see frequently from the car window as we drive into Shropshire. Most days in winter the view is pleasant but unremarkable. Early in the year there is no leaf cover and the structure of the trees is revealed, but the tree trunks themselves are only noticeable as general silhouettes. Then, suddenly, late in the afternoon, the cloud breaks at the horizon to send a shaft of bright light from a leaden sky. The piercing, golden light illuminates the silver, black and mossy green of the birch trunks as if they were on a theatre stage under a spotlight. The contrast of the warm yellow light with the dark, threatening, charcoal grey of the sky is amazing. Colours and patterns that were invisible in the trees and hedgerows are instantly revealed. Occasionally there is even the added drama of a rainbow. The visual impact of the view is transformed and transfixing, making it a miracle we don't drive into a nearby ditch!

There may be no easy way to control the lighting of an outdoor subject other than to wait for nature to take its course. You might decide to rise early to catch a particularly romantic, misty landscape scene or perhaps waiting until sunset would be more interesting. The bright sunlight in the middle of the day sharpens colours, highlights every

TIP Old paintings can provide inspiration for composition and colour. The beautiful flower studies of 17th century Dutch masters, for instance, or the way Vermeer used directional lighting from a side window to illuminate his figures. Notice what the artist has used to surround and frame the main focus of the paintings, too. The background colours and textures are almost as important as those of the objects in the still life and contribute greatly to the overall composition.

Collage of images on a sketchbook page.

detail and provides fantastic shadows. If you are working indoors, from a still life for instance, it is easier to control artificial lighting to introduce drama to the objects in the arrangement. A strong light from one direction is often most effective. A single source of light creates interesting shadows, which in turn emphasizes the connection the objects have to the surface on which they sit. It also heightens the effects of the colours and colour values involved in the arrangement.

Shapes and angles

As you are taking photographs of your subject, decide what are its most interesting shapes. How do you intend to draw attention to those particular shapes? What would happen if you photographed at really close quarters? Would taking the picture from an unpredictable angle help the composition? Would a silhouette be dramatic? It might attract unwelcome attention from your neighbours, but crouching down low to shoot up at the plants in the vegetable plot produces impressively towering subjects.

Texture and line

Texture can be used in a design to add subtle interest to the surface. This might be the visual texture contributed by printed fabric patterns and the variegated effects of hand dyes, or the tactile texture created by continuous free motion quilting using patterns appropriate to the theme of the quilt. It is hard to capture texture accurately in a photograph unless the image is viewed at very close quarters. Really good lighting conditions help define texture on a surface. The strong midday sun shows every detail of a rusted metal door with tiny areas of peeling paint casting harsh shadows.

Line can be photographed in so many ways. It might be the horizon in a landscape or seascape, the verticals and horizontals of walls, windows, rooftops and doorways of a building, or bare branches and twigs seen against a clear, wintry sky.

creative focus As photo editing at home is becoming more commonplace, computer literate quilters can adapt their own photographs. We can remove unnecessary distractions and zoom in on any area to add emphasis or create a new focal point. Even a basic paint program is capable of manipulating colour, mirror imaging and performing cut and paste actions with the simple click of the mouse. Speed isn't always a positive thing, though. Playing with bits of cut or torn paper, arranging photographs, photocopies and prints, adding layers of colour with paint or crayon and other hands-on processes can provide the thinking time needed to resolve a design idea.

Sketchbook page showing photograph with pencil drawing. When we use a photograph in a sketchbook we often crop it or paint areas out with an opaque, acrylic paint to accentuate the contour we want to be most conspicuous in the design. For instance, cutting along a roofline or around an archway or, as here, painting out the background from around the top of the pears.

Drawing

Although there are methods that might be considered tricks and cheats (and we use all of them regularly and without restraint), drawing remains the most important means of recording what we observe from a source of inspiration. There is something about the process of drawing that involves the whole person, both the physical action of the body and the intellect. To draw an object involves making decisions and making comparisons. The marks of a drawing are all relative to each other and require spatial awareness.

Photocopy of painted crow collaged to page with oil pastel drawing and watercolour wash.

Pencil drawing of a crow.

As you draw, there are important questions you should ask yourself to help you put the right sort of mark in the right place on the paper. Firstly, how will the subject fit the available space of the page? Should it fill the paper or be placed in a particular area for the sake of effective composition? How big is the subject in relation to any other objects you also want to depict? Decide whether it lies in front of, or behind, other objects, whether it is darker or lighter than the things that surround it and whether it has shadows and highlights showing the direction of light falling on the surface. Drawing makes you see what is actually there rather than what you think is there!

Drawing materials

Many people claim they can't draw but drawing for design is about being able to convey relevant visual information about the subject, not necessarily about creating a fantastic work of fine art worthy of display on a wall! Anyone able to hold a pencil or, better still, a fat oil pastel can draw. Actually, in the hands of a nervous drawer, a pencil is the most dispiriting and depressing tool as the marks tend to be feeble and timid unless you have the confidence and experience to draw with strong gestures.

An artists' quality oil pastel doesn't let anyone be timid! Good oil pastels release their generous, buttery colour on to the paper effortlessly, especially on a warm day. The beauty of oil pastels is that they make bold marks – it isn't possible to be too intricate or delicate as you can't sharpen them to a point. Oil pastels also resist water-based colours which means washes of drawing ink, watercolour paints or dilute acrylics can be flooded over the drawing without lifting or disturbing any of the pastel colour (see pages 26–27 and 44–45 for more on using pastels).

Using paper with a textured surface also helps make drawings more interesting. The colour picks up on the raised areas, emphasizing the texture of the paper and fragmenting the pastel marks. Although there are lots of heavy quality art papers and proprietary pastel papers available, the 'wrong' side of brown parcel paper works beautifully for pastel drawings. The knowledge that this is such a basic commodity probably makes a novice feel less anxious about the drawing than if a more expensive paper was used. Does it really matter if you have a disaster? It's just a bit of paper! We encourage students to work into drawings with additional layers of colour if they feel a drawing isn't working but if you truly believe it can't be redeemed, paint over it and start again.

Many sketchbook pages are successful because they combine different media and techniques rather than rely on a single product or process. Prepare to experiment to discover what medium or combination of media gives the effect you most enjoy.

Photocopy of a pear painting with additional drawing and handwritten text.

Watercolour painting on top of a screen-printed page.

"Drawing for design is the means to the end, not the end itself."

creative focus The examples here show how Laura creates potential quilt designs on her sketchbook pages. Each separate element of the page is in itself simple – a line, a shape, a patch of colour. It is the way they are placed together, with consideration for contrast, value and scale that creates the decorative effect. Notice how she often creates a collage-like arrangement of shapes, textures and glimpses of text to form a background to her drawing and painting. Looking at these pages, it would be difficult not to imagine how the quilts might evolve. The watercolours could be hand-dyed fabrics, each defined shape could be an appliqué, every line could be a row of machine quilting and every dot and blemish on the skin of the pear might become a bead or a French knot.

Making a Simple Collage

The term collage derives from the French verb coller and simply means to glue. Collage can be a quick and easy method of getting an idea down on paper, involving bits of cut or torn paper glued to a page of a sketchbook. The paper pieces could be taken from newspapers and magazines, recycled from greetings cards and letters or created by painting, photocopying or photographing appropriate subjects. It is perfectly possible to look at a photograph and work immediately with fabrics, but collages are a quick and cheap way to explore what would happen if the number of strips, their measurements, angles and proportions were changed. This is great if you intend working on a series as a number of similar compositions can be produced quickly. In Chapter 9 we will show you how some of our collages were developed to become finished quilts.

TIP Washes of transparent colour can help integrate many different materials and soften colours in the same way that a layer of organza integrates and modifies the fabric patches in shadow appliqué. Anyone who can make crazy patchwork or appliqué has the ability to make collage!

What you need
- *Photo of a landscape*
- *Tracing paper*
- *Pencil*
- *Glue*

1 Select a photograph of an attractive landscape. Place a sheet of tracing paper over the image and draw the most significant lines and shapes with a pencil or fine liner pen. Don't be afraid to simplify the lines and to eliminate some entirely if you feel the design would benefit – you can add more detail later if you decide it is needed. The type of lines you trace may influence the choice of technique you will use to interpret the design into fabric. Patchwork will be easier to construct if the lines of the design are straight or only gently curved. More complicated shapes, acute points and tight curves might be better tackled with appliqué techniques or by printing or stencilling.

2 Number each shape on the tracing so you can identify the order in which the shapes will be placed. Make a copy of the tracing to be your guide. Cut each shape of the original tracing along the pencil lines. Refer to your original source of inspiration to identify colours and colour values.

3 For each of the pattern pieces, select a suitable scrap of paper. Placing each pattern piece on top of the appropriate part of the original image will help you choose the best paper for the collage. Remember, it is the value of each colour that will help convey a convincing impression of foreground and distance.

4 On the chosen paper, draw around the pattern piece with a pencil and cut the shape out. Position each piece of paper referring to the copy tracing and glue in place on a page of your sketchbook.

Landscape inspiration with collage and traced pattern piece shapes. Although the collage has just a few very basic shapes, they still manage to convey the idea of a landscape.

We like to include fragments of text and photographs and then to add more layers of colour, shape or line by printing, painting or drawing on top of the collaged surface.

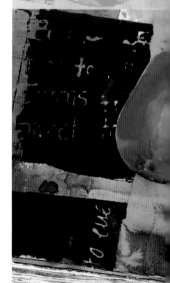

A series of thumbnail collages explore proportion and colour.

Printing

We often try to identify shapes or simple motifs from our design source so that we can use them to create print blocks. Once made, the print block can be used over and over again to explore the potential of repeat patterns, to produce designs for borders or in more informal arrangements for an all-over effect. Working direct to the sketchbook page, we vary the colour of the paint and also that of the paper surface it is used on so that a variety of different colour combinations can be quickly auditioned. Any of the designs we like can then be recreated on fabric using the appropriate products. It often takes only a few minutes, or even seconds, to make a print block. There are lots of suitable materials available from art suppliers or, like us, you can also make use of items found around the home.

TIP Sticky-backed foam sheets can be easily cut to shape with scissors, the paper backing removed and the shapes attached to a cardboard base. A thin layer of acrylic paint will seal the card and make it more durable.

A selection of well-used print blocks.

Polystyrene
This material is ideal for making simple prints. You can buy sheets from an art supply store or recycle suitable grocery packaging. The design is scored into the flat surface with a stylus or ballpoint pen. For anyone nervous of drawing freehand, it is possible to trace over the lines of a photocopy. By pressing quite firmly with the point of the pen, the lines will appear as indentations on the polystyrene surface below the paper. If any of the lines are incomplete, score them with the pen again once the photocopy is removed. Bear in mind that the marks made in the polystyrene will not print – it is what remains of the surface that holds the colour, not the voided channels that have been removed. This means the overall shape of the polystyrene sheet should be taken into consideration. The polystyrene is often rectangular – does that suit the design or would it be better cut to a square or circle? Once a block is prepared, it is such a quick way to try out different arrangements of repeat shapes and the bonus is that the block works just as well on fabric as it does on the pages of a sketchbook.

Wooden print blocks
We sometimes buy lovely little wooden print blocks. We find that the best prints with these are achieved using good quality acrylic paint, but not too

Prints from a foam block.

Bleach print using compressed sponge on a page painted with black fountain pen ink.

much of it. We always recommend trying out a few prints on a scrap of paper before doing a more considered design on paper or fabric. If the channels of the block become clogged with paint they will make indistinct prints; be prepared to wash them and pat them dry on kitchen paper frequently as you work. An old toothbrush is useful for getting paint out of narrow channels.

Compressed craft sponge

This is probably our favourite printing medium. The sheets of sponge are thin and firm when purchased, feeling almost like cardboard. They cut readily with scissors making even complex shapes easy to handle. When placed in water, the cut sponge swells in thickness, becoming soft and pliable. To use them, squeeze the shapes to remove excess water and then dip into acrylic or fabric paint on a palette or old saucer. The thickness of fabric paints does vary so it is always a good idea to make a test print on a scrap of paper before working on anything more precious. As long as the quantity of paint is well judged, the holes of the sponge will be visible in the print shape, adding lots of visual texture. Overloading the sponge with paint fills the holes and the prints lose their lovely bubbles. Compressed sponge works beautifully with bleach on paper that has been coloured with water-soluble media and with discharge paste on fabrics that have been dyed with Procion MX dyes.

Printing with acrylic paint on paper using a self-adhesive foam block.

Oil Pastel and Wash

Rubbings (sometimes referred to as frottage) with a wash of wet media work on the principle that oil and water don't mix! Making an oil pastel rubbing from a wooden print block on to brown parcel paper is a good introduction to the medium. The rubbing can then be painted with a wash of watercolour in a strongly contrasting colour. Wax crayons can be substituted for oil pastels but won't have the same soft, luscious consistency. Some degree of firmness can be an advantage, however, and the very best artists' quality pastels can be too soft to make well-defined rubbings.

Rubbings of textured surfaces are a good way to introduce visual texture to a sketchbook design, which will relate closely to the hand-dyed fabrics used in our quilts. We particularly like to rub pages with the side of a white or iridescent pastel before washing over with a generous layer of watercolour or ink. The pastel enhances the texture of the paper and adds visual interest to an otherwise boring area of flat colour.

TIP When applying a wash to the rubbing, remember that the effect will rely on the contrast of colour between the two media. Using a generous wash of wet colour over the rubbing will cause the paint to pool against the barrier formed by the line of oil pastel, preventing the liquid from flowing any further. As a result, it will dry with a slightly greater density of colour against the edge of the pastel mark.

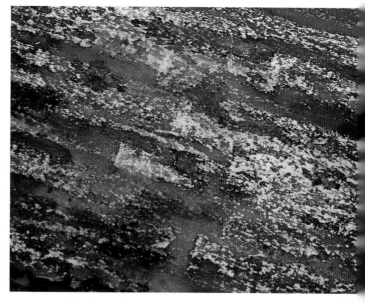

Oil pastel rubbed over textured paper with a wash of dye added. Sketchbook pages with visual texture relate closely to the hand-dyed fabrics of our quilts and so convey our design intentions better than flat colour.

Oil pastels and wax crayons.

materials focus

Rubbings and drawings on fabric can be made in exactly the same way using fabric pastels or Markal Paintstiks instead of oil pastels. The rubbings can be made on to previously dyed fabrics or once the pastel is fixed the fabric can be hand-dyed or painted. See pages 44–45 for examples of rubbings taken from wire shapes.

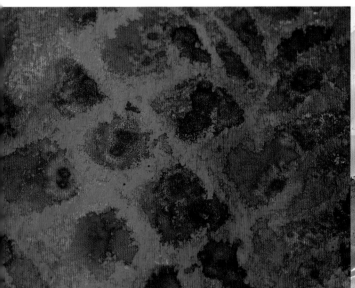

Oil pastel rubbing with ink wash.

We also use oil pastels to make sketches, adding a watery wash of ink, dye or, as in this case, watercolour paint, to create the suggestion of form.

Stencilling on Paper

Paper masks make simple but effective stencils for use with pastels and you don't have to be able to draw to produce great results. Stencils are an excellent method of recording the design element shape. The example here was made by scanning a single floret taken from a garden hydrangea, enlarging the image in a basic computer paint program, printing it on to copy paper and carefully cutting out the shape with scissors. Equally good results could be achieved using a photograph or magazine picture and a photocopier. If you print several copies or save the image on your computer, you can make more stencils as you need them. The flower stencil has been used with artists' soft pastels direct to the pages of a sketchbook. The pastel was applied to the stencil, not the page, and dragged across the cut edge and into the aperture with a fingertip. Moving the stencil and repeating the process produces overlapping shapes with the same delicate appearance as the original source of inspiration.

TIP This technique is a quick way to try out a variety of colour combinations and compositions before working a favoured design on to fabric. Try a single motif, a border of slightly overlapping shapes or repeat the motif several times to create multiple images.

Unless you intend to make a quilt with a lot of white fabric in it, stencilling on to paper that has already been painted with a wash of watercolour or dilute acrylic paint is the best way to make your design work look as the finished quilt might.

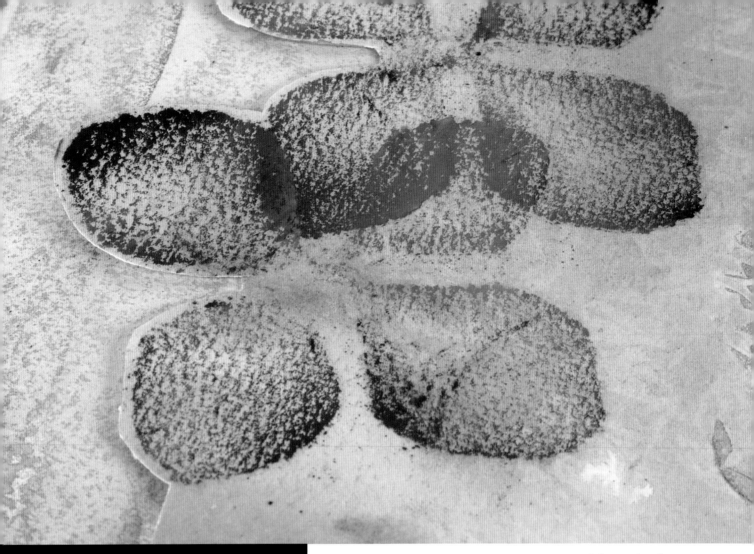

Soft pastels enhance the texture of the paper on which they are used. Distressing the paper by crumpling it in your hand before applying the pastel can look fantastic.

Stencil made from a scanned hydrangea floret.

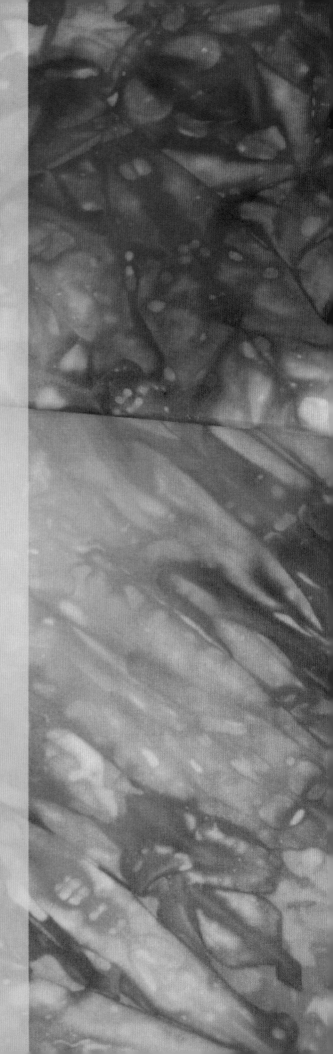

What Fabric? What Colour?

In this chapter we will look at what fabrics to use and how to prepare them for a variety of product applications. You will also find basic recipes for the dyes, related solutions and pastes that you will need to carry out the techniques we describe throughout the book. Some of the techniques and products we mention are suitable for all types of fabric but others are more specific. For an 'at a glance' reminder of what to use with what, refer to the chart on page 35. Most of the techniques we use will work well on natural fibres such as cotton, linen and silk.

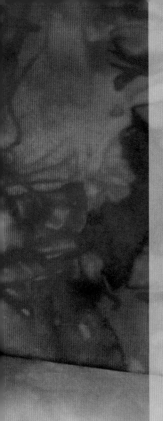

Health and safety

Previous page: Hand-dyed fabrics.

Basic equipment.

It is essential to observe sensible and safe practice when handling any chemical products in the home, classroom or studio. Procion MX dyes (see pages 36–37) are considered non-toxic but you should avoid inhaling all dye powders and associated chemicals. Wear rubber gloves and a mask when mixing solutions. To reduce the risk of fine powder being released into the atmosphere, dyes should always be added to water rather than water poured on to dye. If you have respiratory problems or are pregnant, ask someone else to mix your solutions or consider using ready-mixed fabric paints and liquid dyes. A sheet of damp newspaper placed on the work surface will collect stray particles of dye that might be floating in the air and makes cleaning up simple. All tools and equipment should be dedicated to fabric dyeing use only and kept away from food preparation areas. Manufacturers will supply product safety guidelines if requested, or you can refer to their websites for detailed information.

TIP Tearing soda-treated fabric can release particles into the air where they may cause a reaction in those who are sensitive. For this reason, always cut soda-soaked fabrics with scissors or a rotary cutter.

Fabrics printed with thickened dyes.

fabric focus If you intend over-dyeing a fabric that is already coloured, remember that the normal rules of colour mixing will apply. Dye colour is transparent and cannot completely cover an existing colour. For instance, if you dye yellow fabric blue, the result will tend more to green than blue.

Fabric choices

Cotton: We prefer mercerised cotton poplin for any of the techniques involving Procion dyes. This has a high thread count, a smooth surface and is brilliant white, meaning any dye colour we add to it will remain clear and bright too. Every other technique we discuss in the book will also work on this fabric.

Linen: Although not so commonly available, linen is a lovely material for quiltmakers. It takes dye beautifully and is really receptive to quilting. The easiest types to work with are lightweight, finely woven and relatively smooth.

Silk: Although silk is of animal origin and therefore a protein fibre, it can be dyed successfully with the same Procion MX dyes that are more commonly used for cellulose fibres. Silk is available in a wide range of weights and textures. The thinnest Habotai weight may be too insubstantial for patchwork but, like the medium and heavyweight silks, is very successful for quilting.

Textured fabrics: Textured fabrics and those with interesting weave patterns may produce exciting effects but make sure the surface suits the chosen technique. A textured fabric would give a broken effect to a print, for instance, and the fragmentation might distort the subject, making it too indistinct to be recognisable. Some textured fabrics are very absorbent and will be greedy with dye and paint.

Synthetic blends: Bear in mind that fabrics with any synthetic content will not readily accept dyes designed for natural fibres and, although they will take on some colour, the greater the proportion of synthetic content, the paler the results will be. Pastel results when you were expecting intense colour can be very disappointing so it is better to avoid polycotton blends unless you are working with fabric paints and pastels that sit on the surface rather than react with the fibres.

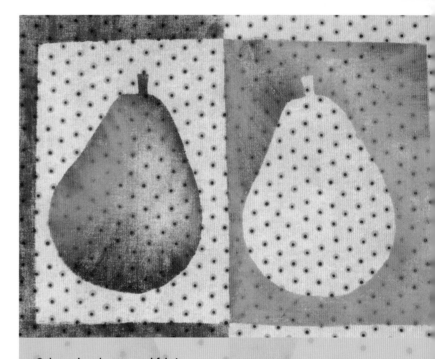

Coloured and patterned fabrics can be very successful with many of the printing methods we use, especially when working with masks and stencils, as this example of Markal stencilling on to a comercially patterned fabric illustrates.

Pretreating Fabrics

Unless fabrics are bought as PFD (prepared for dyeing) they should be washed before use as they probably have a surface treatment, which may inhibit penetration of dye and paint. If in any doubt about the fabric you are using, machine wash with detergent before applying any colour. All natural fibres need to be soaked in a soda solution before dyeing, painting or printing them with fibre-reactive Procion dyes, even if they are sold as PFD. Sodium carbonate or soda ash is the fixative needed to ensure that Procion MX dye reacts with the fibres of the cloth and makes a permanent bond. Washing soda sold in supermarkets can be substituted for soda ash, but it might contain bleaching agents and may not give quite such reliable results as pure sodium carbonate.

1 To make a soda solution, use three scant tablespoons of soda ash (or 200g of washing soda) to a litre of hot water. Follow individual manufacturer's guidelines if these vary from the above. Soda solution can be stored in airtight plastic or glass containers until required. Allow to cool to room temperature before using.

2 If you intend to dye fabric using low water immersion techniques (see pages 36–37), the dye and soda solutions can be added at the same time. For all other applications, place the fabric in a quantity of soda solution and allow it to sit submerged for a minimum of 20 minutes. Agitate it from time to time to ensure the fibres are completely saturated. Lift the fabric with gloved hands and squeeze as much of the solution back into the container as possible (a funnel will help).

Special effects with dyes on cotton fabrics.

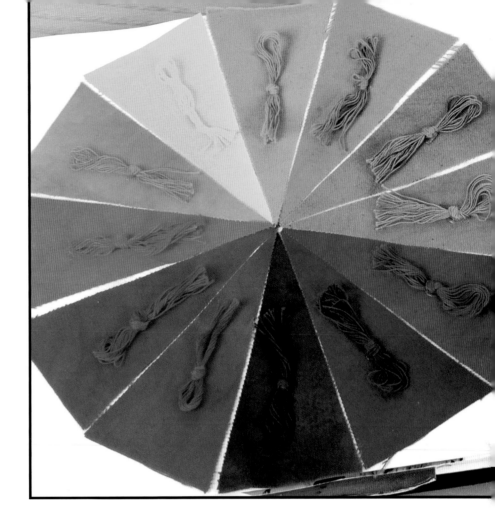

Hand-dyed fabrics and threads arranged in a colour wheel.

3 Line dry the fabric out of doors or allow to drip dry over a plastic tray. A short spin in a washing machine can speed up the drying, but make sure no rinse cycle is involved as this would remove the soda solution from the fabric.

4 Soda-soaked fabric can be used while still damp for some techniques, but bear in mind that the edges of colour applied to damp fabric will bleed rather than remain sharp. If clear definition is preferred, allow the fabric to dry completely, then iron on a medium setting using a dry iron.

Soda-soaked cotton and linen fabrics can be stored until needed but, as lengthy contact of soda ash with silk fibres can cause damage, it is advisable to use treated silk immediately. Leftover soda solution will keep for ages (as long as dye hasn't been added to it) and it can be reused.

Process	Fabric type	Presoak with soda?	Heat fix?	Rinse?
Stencilling with fabric pastels	Any	No	Yes	No
Printing with fabric paint	Any	No	Yes	No
Printing with acrylic paint	Any	No	No	No
Painting with fabric paint	Any	No	Yes	No
Drawing with fabric pens	Any	No	Maybe	No
Spraying with fabric paint	Any	No	Yes	No
Printing with thickened dyes	Cotton, linen silk, viscose rayon	Yes	No	Yes
Transferring colour with painted fusible	Any that can stand sufficient heat from the iron	No	Yes	No
Removing colour with bleach	Cotton, linen	No	No	Yes
Removing colour with discharge paste	Cotton, linen	No	Yes	Yes
T-Shirt transfer images	Any	No	Yes	No

Table of pretreatments required for processes and fabric types.

Low Water Immersion Dyeing

Almost all of our quilts start life as cotton, linen and silk fabrics, which we hand-dye with Procion MX fibre-reactive dyes. We don't follow exact recipes for dye solutions, preferring instead to judge the strength of colour by eye, just as an artist would when painting a picture. Hand-dyeing is fundamental to the look we want for our fabrics and we keep the technique we use as simple as possible. Known as low water immersion dyeing, this is the process we use.

What you need

- Procion MX dyes
- Small glass jars
- Soda ash solution
- Plastic containers
- Rubber gloves

Red Procion dye powder.

Blue Procion dye powder.

1 First make a concentrated Procion dye solution. In a small container such as a jam jar, mix approximately half a teaspoon of dye powder with just enough warm water to make a smooth paste. Stir until all the dry powder is in the solution. You're aiming to produce a strong smooth paste that can be diluted for basic dyeing techniques, but can also be added to sodium alginate paste (see pages 38–39) without making it too thin for printing. Keep a lid on the container until you are ready to work.

2 Pour a quantity of soda ash solution on to damp fabrics that are crumpled into small, plastic containers (ice cream tubs are perfect). Squeeze the fabric with gloved hands to ensure it is completely saturated with the solution. Leave it to soak through.

3 Meanwhile, place two or three spoonfuls of concentrated dye solution into a clean jar and add a little more water to dilute it. Repeat this process with a separate jar for each colour you intend to use.

4 Add two or three spoonfuls of dye solution into the plastic container containing the cloth and let them merge gently with the wet fabric to create interesting colour mixes. You can squeeze the fabric gently to help distribute the colour but we try not to open or manipulate the creases very much as this tends to produce too homogenous a result for our taste. You can experiment for the effects you prefer. The tighter the fabric is

materials focus Procion MX dyes are fibre-reactive colours used in cold water dye processes where they react with natural fibres of cotton, linen, viscose, rayon and silk. Fabrics must be treated with a soda ash solution to ensure the colour becomes permanent (see page 34–35). Dye solutions can be made thin, like water, or thick, like a paste, depending on how they are to be used. Thin solutions will flow and spread on the cloth with colours mixing and merging, especially if the fabric is already wet. Dye solutions thickened with sodium alginate (see page 38–39) will tend to remain where they are put, making them ideal for printing methods where a more defined edge is desired. Dyes are very concentrated and a little goes a long way.

TIP Colours always appear darker when wet than they will once the fabric is dry and most of the subtleties in the patterning will only reveal themselves when the fabric is ironed.

Yellow Procion dye powder.

packed into the container and the less handling it gets, the more separate the colours will remain and the more pronounced the patterning of colour. An understanding of basic colour theory is useful to predict the colours you will create by mixing dyes. If you have trouble anticipating what will happen, you can dip a paintbrush into the mixed dye and paint a little on paper to preview the effect. Adding too many colours will usually make mud!

5 After a minimum of an hour (often longer), rinse the fabrics in cold water until all the excess colour runs clear and, finally, machine wash at 40C.

Once dry the fabrics are now prepared and ready to receive any of the painting and printing techniques that we describe in the following pages.

Making Thick Dye Pastes

Sodium alginate is a seaweed-based product, which swells in contact with water and can be used to make Procion MX dye solutions thick enough for a range of painting and printing techniques. Known by various brand names around the world, sodium alginate is readily available from suppliers of dyestuffs. Rather like making wallpaper paste, the granules of sodium alginate are mixed with a little water and allowed to stand until thick and smooth. The thickness of the paste can be adjusted by adding more or less granules in ratio to water, as required for the chosen purpose.

Sodium alginate paste

materials focus It is impossible to be exact about specific quantities of sodium alginate to use, as product characteristics vary from one manufacturer to another. Be prepared to experiment to arrive at the most suitable thickness of paste. More of that in Chapter 7.

Dye paste for printing

To make a thick paste for mono printing, screen printing and block printing, add approximately four tablespoons of sodium alginate to three cups of water. Whisk vigorously for several minutes and then allow to stand for four hours, or even overnight, until you have a smooth paste and any lumps have dissolved. This stock solution can be stored in an airtight container in a cool place for several days. When you are ready to print, add a little concentrated dye solution to the stock paste in a clean container.

You can judge the colour value of the mix by brushing a tiny amount on to a sheet of white kitchen paper. Remember, the colour will appear darker and brighter when

it is wet than when it has dried on the fabric, but it does give some indication of whether you have added enough dye to the paste.

Dye paste for painting

Dye painting is the application of thickened dye direct to the fabric surface. It can be applied with a brush, roller, sponge, knife or squeezy bottle. Because the dye is thickened, the marks of the tools used to apply it remain visible after the fabric is cured and washed, introducing interesting visual texture.

Dye painting can use the same thickness of paste as that suggested for printing (above), but it is quite likely

you will prefer a thinner mix as this will encourage the colour to flow more readily on the surface of the fabric. Just add a little extra water until the desired consistency is achieved. Like any painting technique, this is a matter of personal preference – some artists love to paint wet on wet while others prefer dry brush techniques.

Decanting paint paste into a plastic squeezy bottle that has a small nozzle helps produce fine lines and is ideal for text. Place the nozzle so that it touches the surface of the fabric and draw or write whilst squeezing the bottle to extrude the colour. To keep the lines narrow, use a small nozzle and thick paste colour that won't spread too much.

Stock paste with dye added. Only combine dye and paste when you are ready to paint or print, as mixing the two together begins the reactive process and shortens the effective shelf life of the mixture.

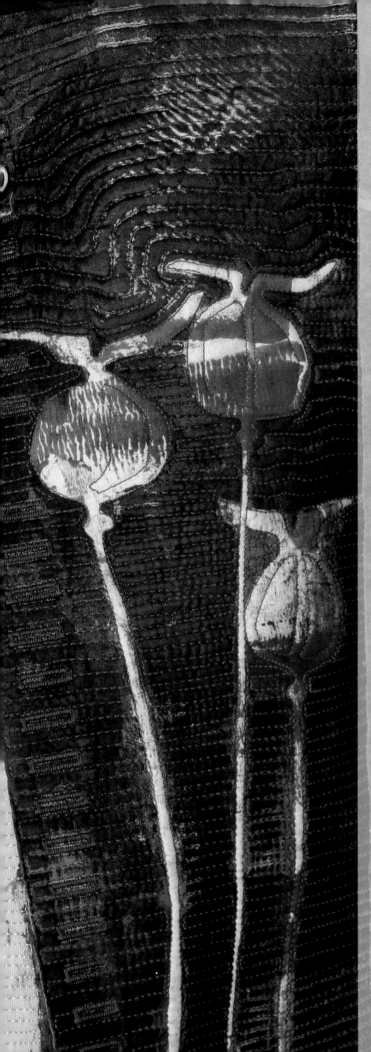

Colour Before Quilting

There is a bewildering array of products and techniques than can be used to apply colour to a fabric surface. We are going to talk about a few of our favourites in this chapter. We like to keep things as simple as we can. We especially love monoprinting for its immediacy, stencilling for the degree of control it affords and block printing for sheer speed. Screen printing is a perfect method of producing numerous repeats of a single design and rubbings have their own unique quality.

Stencilling on Fabric

Playing on paper with different colours of soft pastel and different arrangements of simple shapes will soon produce a design that you will want to use in a quilt. The translation of the process is straightforward, simply requiring you to substitute fabric pastels in place of soft pastels and fabric instead of paper. Smooth, close weave, 100% cotton fabrics are the easiest to work with but fabric pastels will work on a wide range of fabrics. Check the packaging of your product for specific information.

Previous page: *Metamorphosis* by Laura.

TIP Used paper stencils get covered in pastel and old toothbrushes become stained. Sometimes serendipity makes lovely colour mixes but, if it is important to maintain colour purity, use a clean stencil and brush for each application.

Hydrangea Hanging.

What you need

- *Fabric pastels (we use Markal Paintstiks)*
- *Fabric*
- *Paper stencil*
- *Baking parchment*
- *Iron*

Markal Paintstiks are sealed with a protective skin which reforms after use; the skin has to be taken off each time it is used, easily done by placing the tip of the pastel into crumpled kitchen paper and twisting firmly.

1 Place a piece of fabric on a firm work surface. We make sure that the fabric is taut by taping it to the table with a little masking tape at each corner.

2 Scribble a generous amount of fabric pastel on to the stencil near to the edge of the shape (**a**).

3 Drag the colour off the stencil, across the edge of the paper and on to the fabric (**b**). Many people apply the colour with a fingertip – if you don't like to get your hands dirty you may prefer to use an old toothbrush. It needs a generous amount of pastel and firm pressure to make a strong mark but you can keep applying more pastel until you reach the depth of colour you want. It is important to keep the stencil absolutely still or edges of shapes will blur.

   (As well as taping the fabric down, you could also hold the paper in place by spraying the back with temporary spray adhesive. Alternatively, make the stencil using freezer paper, place the waxy side against the fabric and iron to secure. Remove the stencil before fixing the pastel colour or it will be very difficult to remove later.)

4 Carefully remove the stencil (**c**).

5 After applying the pastel, leave it to cure for 72 hours, then cover with a sheet of baking parchment and fix by ironing with a dry iron. The fixing process may vary between brands of pastel so always read manufacturers' guidelines for usage.

a Applying pastel to stencil.

b Dragging colour into aperture.

c Removing the stencil.

fabric focus Fabric pastels have a transparent quality that allows the colour of the fabric to show through. This means the colour of one pastel will look different depending on the fabric used. For instance, a yellow pastel used on blue fabric will appear green but if used on red fabric will look orange. Compare the difference by using the same pastel across a striped fabric or one pieced from different coloured strips. Hand-dyed, mercerised cotton poplin fabric and a maximum of three pastel colours have been used for the samples shown below.

Rubbings with Fabric Pastels

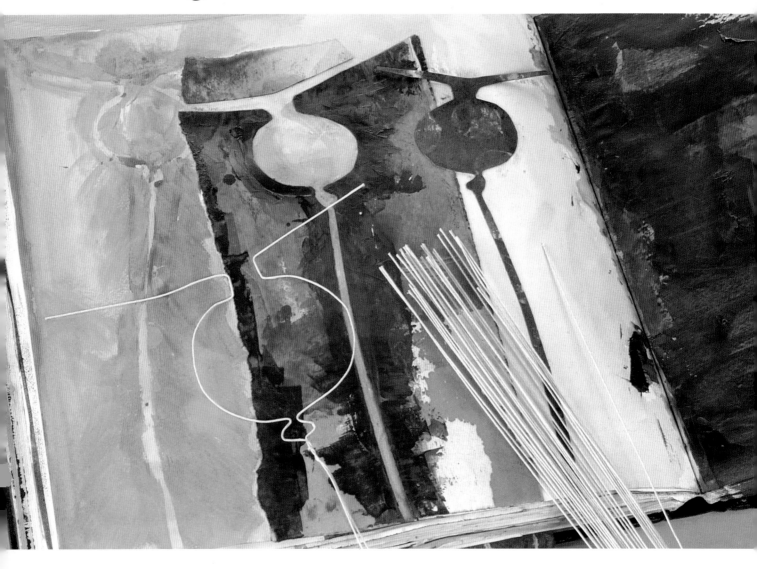

Wire shapes for poppy seedhead rubbings.

Drawing a shape can mean many things, not just making marks with a pencil. Here the contours of a pear and a poppy seed head have been created with wire. Although the wire appears to be very fine, when placed beneath paper or fabric, it creates a raised edge from which a rubbing can be made using an oil pastel on paper or a fabric pastel on cloth. Using rubbings is always a slightly messy technique as edges cannot be defined exactly – accept this as part of the charm! Fabric pastel rubbings on cloth need to be cured for approximately 72 hours and then fixed by ironing.

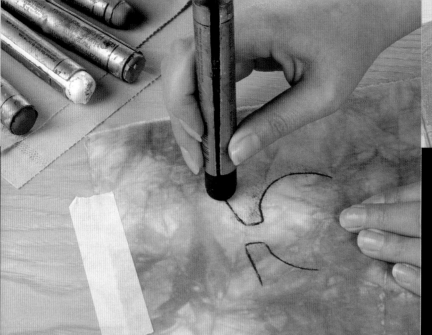

Use the fingers of your free hand to feel where the wire line lies and guide the path of the pastel.

A simple line or shape made using this technique can be fixed and then additional colour or fine detail added with fabric paints or pens – as in this wire rubbing of pears with additional pastel drawing.

materials focus Sugarcraft wire is fine, malleable and, since it is paper coated, will accept dye or paint making it ideal for mixed media projects as well as for rubbings.

Pastel wire rubbing of pear on black fabric.

Block Printing

We talked in Chapter 2 about using block printing to develop design ideas in sketchbooks. Happily, the same tools and techniques are equally successful on fabric with just a few changes to the colouring media used. Block printing involves making direct contact with a tool, coated with paint or thickened dye, on to fabric. The block is recharged with wet colour between prints as necessary. Prints can be carefully registered to build up larger areas of repeat pattern. Lots of different tools can be used and it's a good idea to try a variety out until you find what you like best. Bear in mind that, once dry, acrylic paint needs no further fixing but that fabrics have to be presoaked with soda solution before using thickened dye. Fabric paints are usually ironed to fix.

TIP It takes a little time to carve lino to make a print block but the effort is well worth making. Line blocks are really durable and can be used over and over again. You can also make rubbings of the carved surface.

The bubbles of a compressed printing sponge are visible in the prints, contributing lovely textural marks.

materials focus Artists' plastic erasers are a lovely size to use as a print block for miniature designs or to create complex repeat patterns. They carve easily with a lino-cutting tool. Remember that you must always cut away from the body to avoid accidents with any cutting device; a vice to hold the eraser steady as you carve would be ideal. We draw the design on to the eraser with a pencil or ballpoint pen as a guide for the cutting. Acrylic paint dries quickly and will clog the narrow channels of the print block, so take care to wash the eraser frequently.

A cork dipped in thick household bleach makes lovely marks on black velvet. Stop the action of the bleach with several rinses in clean water followed by a final rinse in sodium thiosulphate solution or use a commercial product such as Anti Clor or Bleach Stop (details of suppliers on page 120).

Simple geometric designs are readily available as wooden printing blocks and are great for making repeat patterns. We use wooden blocks mostly with acrylic paint or with discharge paste (see pages 70–71).

Sketchbook page of prints on paper and fabric.

Acrylic paint prints on discharged fabrics (see pages 70–71).

Basic Screen Printing

Screen-printed beetle, with added stripes (see page 51).

Screen printing can seem daunting and too technical for the novice print maker but we use the technique in its simplest form and love the effects we get. This involves a few specialist items and takes some preparation time but once the equipment is set up, we find it is a very efficient way of making multiple prints really quickly. At its simplest, a silk screen consists of a wooden frame with a sheet of fine polyester mesh stretched taut across it. Some screens also have a flat, wooden base and a small leg that pivots at one side of the frame to hold the screen open between prints. Constructing your own frame means you can make it any size you want but popular sizes are readily available from educational suppliers, craft and art stores. The size of the print possible is determined by the area of the mesh visible once the edges have been taped with masking tape.

You will also need a squeegee (the wooden tool with a flexible rubber blade used to spread the print paste across the screen). Make sure the squeegee fits comfortably into the size of frame you choose to work with.

The basic print paste (see pages 38–39) is perfect for screen printing, with the benefit that using thickened dye means the fabric remains just as soft after printing as it was before.

What you need

· A silk screen

· A squeegee

· Soda-soaked fabric
(see pages 34–35)

· A quantity of basic print
paste (see pages 38–39)

· Masking tape

· Paper stencil

· Newspapers or drop sheet
to protect the work area

· Sheets of plastic or
recycle large plastic refuse/
carrier bags

Trial screen print on newspaper and sketchbook page.

Placing thickened dye at top of the screen.

1 To prepare the screen for the first
print, mask the edges of the mesh with
decorators' masking tape. This will create
a nice, straight edge to the print. Place a
sheet of soda-treated fabric beneath the
frame and secure with more tape. Make
sure the fabric is smooth and taut.

2 Position a paper stencil or mask to fit
centrally within the edges of the screen.
Closing the screen allows you to check
the stencil is in the best position with an
equal margin surrounding it. It is usually
a good idea to make the first print on a
piece of newspaper, just to make sure
everything is positioned properly before
risking a piece of precious fabric – see
picture above.

3 Spoon two or three tablespoons of print
paste at the top edge of the closed
frame as shown (**a**).

TIP By introducing different
colours each time a print is made,
the same stencil can be used to
produce many variations of the
original. Colours will mix and
merge on the screen, sometimes
in an unpredictable way.

4 Drag the colour across the screen pressing firmly with the squeegee (**b**). Ask a friend to hold the frame steady if it helps to have both hands free to make the print. The paste may not spread evenly first time; after the first print has been made, the mesh will be wet and coverage will be more even. If some areas of the screen don't seem to be fully covered with dye, scoop up the excess paste that will now be at the bottom of the screen and repeat the process.

Spreading the dye with a squeegee.

5 Lift the screen (**c**) and remove the tape holding the fabric.

6 Place the print on a plastic bag and cover immediately with a second sheet of plastic.

TIP After step 6, the stencil you used will now be firmly adhered to the underside of the screen. You can therefore make as many additional prints of the same design as you want until you run out of paste or fabric!

Lifting the screen to reveal the print.

fabric focus At the end of the session, roll the stack of prints loosely and leave, enclosed in a plastic bag, at room temperature for at least four hours – longer is fine. After this time, rinse the prints with copious quantities of cool water to remove any excess paste. Once the water runs clear, machine wash the prints at 40° with detergent. They are now ready for drying and ironing.

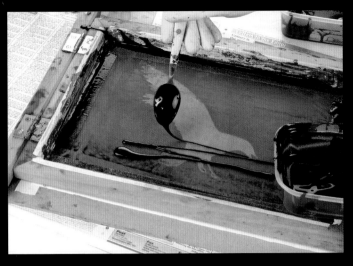

creative focus Breaking most of the accepted
rules of how to apply the colour to a screen printing
frame can produce some exciting effects as in the
striped beetle shown on page 48. Try dropping blobs
or drizzles of paste across the screen instead of only
at the top edge of the frame, as shown above left and
above right.

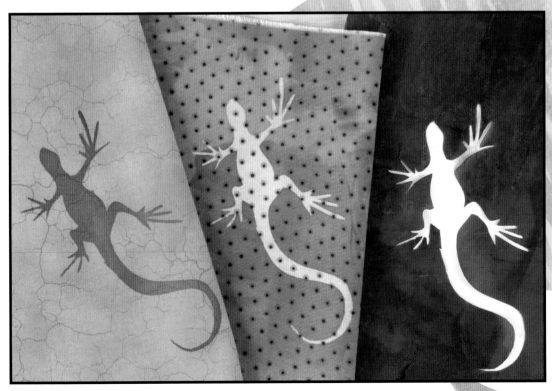

**Try screen printing the
same design on to a
variety of comercially
printed fabrics.**

Monoprinting

As the name suggests, monoprinting produces a single image. This is our absolute favourite printing technique! It is a speedy process that works equally well on paper and fabric. Dye is spread thinly on a plastic sheet, then marked using one of a great variety of tools. These marks are then transferred to the paper or fabric.

You can make monoprints on paper using the same basic print paste as for fabric, or you could substitute any acrylic paint. Monoprints transfer such a thin layer of colour into a sketchbook the pages dry really quickly. If you are nervous of conventional drawing, monoprinting is a really liberating technique.

Use any leftover print paste by rolling or painting it on to sketchbook pages. This will add visual texture and provide an interesting background for drawing or collage.

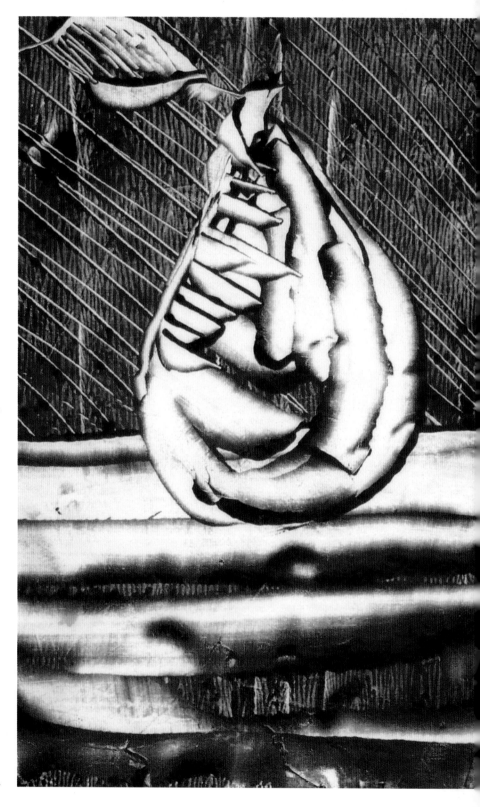

Monoprinted pear.

What you need

- *A sheet of template plastic (available from quilt stores) or thin acetate*
- *A quantity of basic print paste in one or more colours*
- *A brayer or firm sponge roller (a second roller to be kept clean is useful)*
- *Soda-soaked fabric (see Chapter 3)*
- *Sheets of plastic or recycle large, plastic refuse/carrier bags*
- *Kitchen paper towels*
- *Newspapers or a drop sheet to cover and protect the work area*
- *Paintbrushes*
- *Palette knife*
- *Scraps of cardboard*
- *Paper stencils/newspaper/ masking tape/freezer paper*

Different tools make different marks: try brushes, palette knives and combs.

1 To make a monoprint on fabric, apply a thin layer of basic print paste to a sheet of plastic template material or acetate using a roller or brush (**a** and **b**). Notice the texture that is left in the layer of dye – monoprinting is so sensitive to marks that this texture will transfer to your print adding exciting background interest.

Adding colour to the plastic/ acetate with a palette knife.

Spreading colour evenly with a roller.

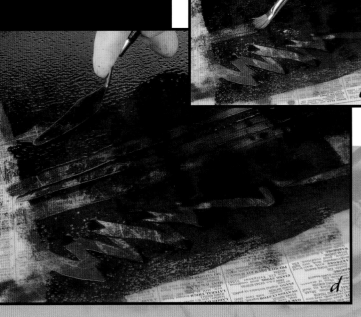

2 Now make additional marks into the wet colour by drawing with a palette knife, the edge of a scrap of card, the wrong end of a paintbrush or any other tool that will push the thickened dye around (**c** and **d**). Take care to wipe any excess colour off the end of the implement with a piece of kitchen paper as each mark is made or the dye will build up and may spoil the next line you make.

Making marks in wet dye with a brush (inset) and a palette knife.

Pressing the fabric on to the wet dye on the plastic/acetate sheet.

e

3 When you are happy with the design, lower a piece of soda-soaked fabric over the plastic/acetate, taking care not to trap air bubbles, and press firmly with a clean roller or the flat of your hands (**e**). You will probably be able to see the colour through the cloth, especially if you are working on white fabric.

4 Peel the fabric away from the plastic/acetate (**f**). Remember that the dye will only bond with the fabric whilst moisture is present – placing a plastic bag or similar over the print will ensure the fabric doesn't dry out before this reaction can be effective (**g**). As you make subsequent prints, stack them with a layer of plastic between each. To keep colours fresh between the prints it may be necessary to clean the plastic/acetate with a piece of kitchen paper.

5 Leave the prints to cure for at least four hours at room temperature, then rinse and wash ready for use. The plastic/acetate can then be rinsed in clean water and dried ready for next time.

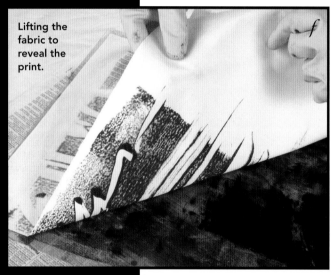

Lifting the fabric to reveal the print.

f

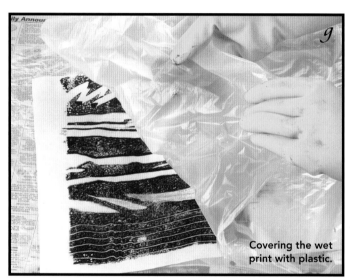

g

Covering the wet print with plastic.

creative focus Experimenting by printing variations of the same simple design side by side, using different methods, results in a striking effect and allows you to directly compare techniques.

First the fabric has been monoprinted with a poppy seed head motif drawn into the dye paste using a palette knife.

Alongside, a further poppy was added by masking the shape with newspaper and printing the background.

Finally, a third motif was added by masking the background area with newspaper and applying the dye paste through the stencil with a sponge roller.

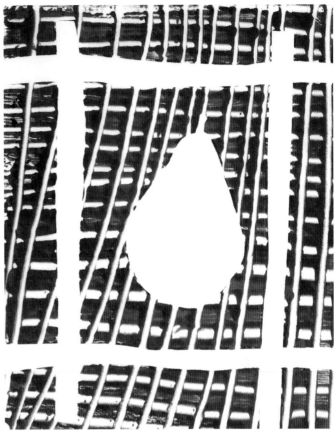

Try making abstract patterns into the layer of wet paste and then carefully position a paper mask on to the plastic/acetate before lowering the fabric. This will print a layer of textured colour on to any area not masked by the paper, as in this pear design.

Narrow strips of cut or torn newspaper are a quick way to make stripes or to create a frame to a design, as here. Just bear in mind that the monoprint will produce the opposite appearance of the mask!

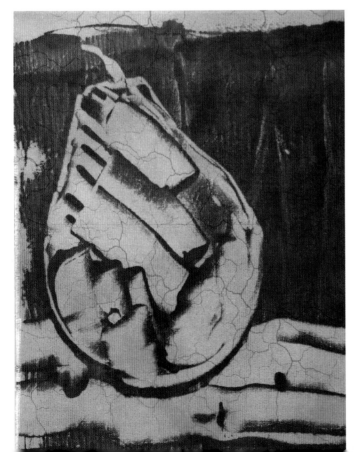

Instead of working on white, try patterned or pale coloured fabrics as a base for prints, as shown in this pear print, or consider over-dyeing the monoprints with a pale colour after the dyes have fixed.

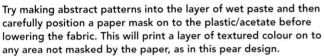

TIP As an alternative to paper masks placed on to the paint-covered plastic/acetate, cut shapes from freezer paper and iron them to the right side of the fabric before making the print.

fabric focus When working on large pieces of fabric it is usually easier to position the print exactly by flipping the plastic/acetate on to the fabric rather than by lowering the fabric on to the acetate.

Colour After Quilting

When most people would consider a quilt to be finished, we think the fun is just about to begin! Once we have completed the quilting (and often even after attaching the binding and the hanging sleeve), we then begin to add more colour to the surface of the quilt. These final applications might be confined to a small area or they might be more general, sometimes modifying much of the quilt top. Additional colour can be used to add new design features, to enhance texture or to define shapes identified within the lines of quilting.

Applying Pastel After Quilting

The textured surface of a quilted textile resembles the contours of a landscape in miniature; think of the lines of quilting as the valleys and the raised areas as the mountains. Stroking pastel colour across the quilt emphasizes the texture as colour picks up on the mountains and avoids the valleys. We like to apply the colour direct to the fabric, pressing the pastel to the cloth using quite firm pressure and working in a single direction. Doing this drags the fabric slightly, causing it to crease when it reaches the line of quilting. This results in deposits of extra colour on the edges of the creases, which adds to the interest. Applying the colour using a brush and a back and forth action would drive the colour into the valleys – not the effect we are after! By avoiding the valleys, the original colour of the stitching is maintained, as is a narrow halo of fabric colour either side of the quilting.

Previous page: *Goblin Market*, detail, by Laura.

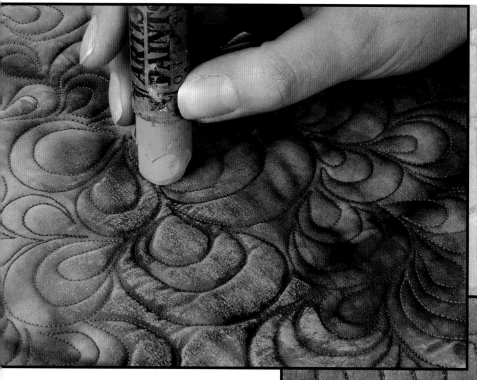

materials focus It can be difficult to imagine how the final fabric surface will appear, so it is important to bear in mind that the eventual effect will depend on several factors. As well as the design of the quilting, the colour of the fabric, that of the quilting thread and, of course, that of the pastel have to be considered carefully. Be sure to maintain colour and/or value contrast between these variables.

The fabric of *Black Moon* was mostly black and white until rose and copper Markal pastels were applied after the quilting was complete.

Fabric pastel picks up on the raised areas of the quilted surface.

The original colour of the quilting thread remains visible after the pastel is applied.

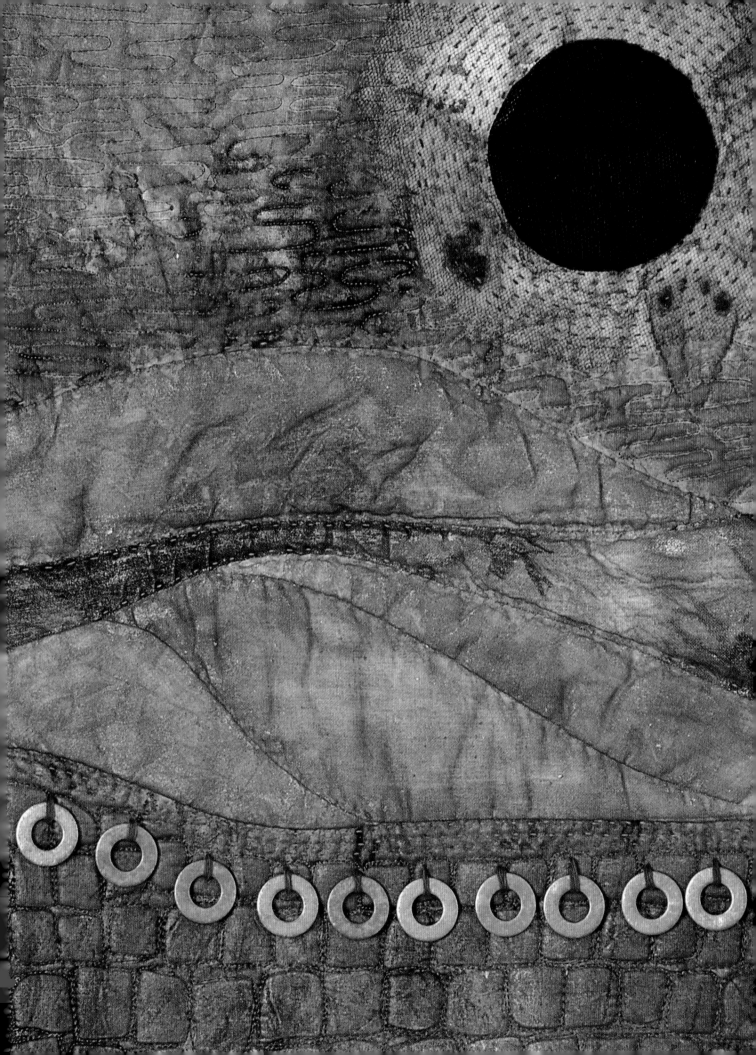

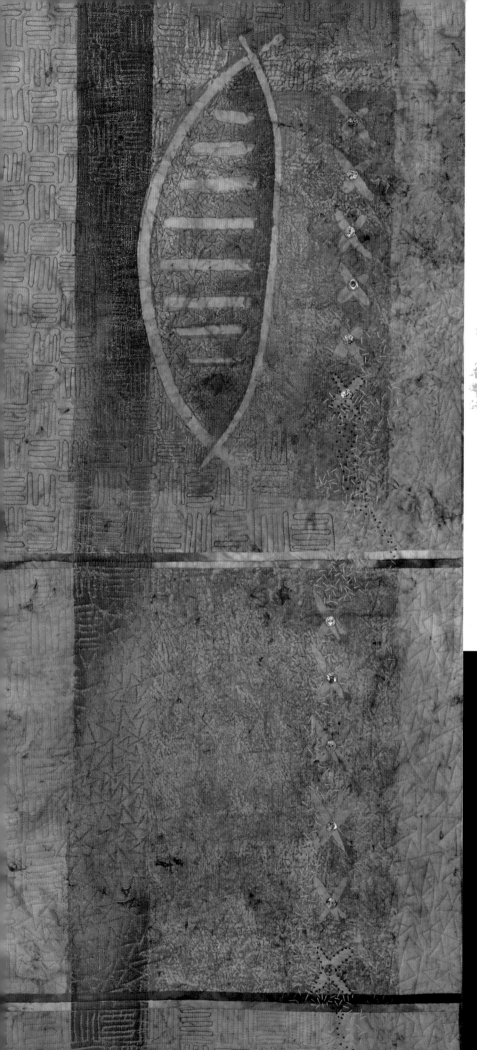

To protect and preserve areas of the quilt that are to retain their original colour, we use masking tape lightly applied to the surface of the quilt. The tape is peeled away as soon as enough pastel has been applied to the area alongside it. A stencil made of freezer paper would serve a similar purpose if the area of pastel colour was intended to be a specific shape, especially for curved or intricate edges. Although freezer paper doesn't leave a residue on the fabric, some masks can stick. For this reason, it is advisable to remove any temporary mask as soon as the stencilling is complete and always before ironing to fix the applied colour.

TIP The lines of quilting need to be spaced quite closely together to achieve the best results for applying pastel. We suggest no more than 2.5cms (1in) apart.

creative focus Linda's quilt, *Spirit*, had an interesting monoprinted shield motif but lacked sufficient focus to be considered finished. The vertical band of dark red and turquoise Markal pastel colour, applied between two strips of masking tape, added drama and weight. Continuing the band across the binding and into the second panel in the lower section of the quilt created a strong visual connection and because the colour was added after quilting, it also accentuated the design of the stitch patterns.

Masking tape was used here to create straight edges to the applied pastel.

Painting After Quilting

Lines of stitching delineate shapes on the quilt surface. The stitches can be made to enclose an area and will form a natural edge to applications of paint. This is an ideal way to introduce colour that will give emphasis to the shape and create a motif that at first glance looks convincingly like appliqué. We use either artists' quality acrylic paint or fabric paint straight from the tube or jar without additional water. If paint is too fluid it is difficult to control bleed at the edge of the painted shape. It is possible, though, to use a more dilute mixture in the centre of a large area of colour if you want to achieve watercolour wash effects or allow some of the base fabric to show through the paint. Colours can be premixed on a palette or allowed to blend on the fabric itself. The paint is left to dry and ironed to fix (if necessary for that particular product).

Rust Never Sleeps **was inspired by the broken glass in an old rusty greenhouse. The painted black shapes reflect the sharp points of the broken shards and are echoed in the angular lines of satin stitch embroidery. The paint used in this instance dried to a soft sheen – appropriate for the original inspiration of metal and glass.**

Applying the paint right up to the stitched line using a small paintbrush.

TIP Identifying interesting shapes in areas of free motion quilting can provide suitable candidates for painting. The shape has to be completely enclosed to provide an edge to the paint.

Where the circles of machine quilting overlap in this sample, narrow ellipses are created. These have been painted with copper metallic paint to accentuate their shape.

Linda's quilt, *Sirens' Call*, has photographic image transfers of Sirens' faces with hair that has been hand-painted with metallic Jacquard Lumiere paints. The shapes of the main painted areas were delineated by the lines of machine quilting, intended to suggest sinuous tendrils of hair floating and flowing under water. Sometimes additional quilting was worked back into the painted shapes after the paint was dry. This creates a different effect to that where the paint is applied up to the stitched line, especially if the colour of thread contrasts strongly with that of the paint.

materials focus Metallic colours cover both light and dark fabrics, either when used on their own to add a lovely gleam, or when mixed with basic colours for more subtle effects. Make sure that if you combine different products they are compatible and have the same method of fixing.

Rollering

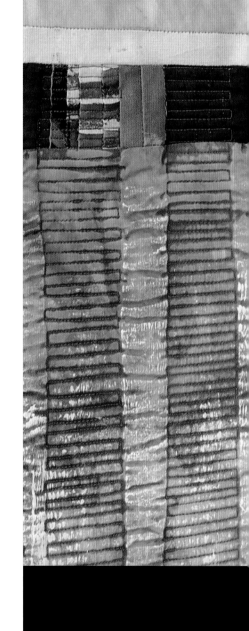

Applying paint to a quilted surface with a sponge roller creates similar effects to those achieved with fabric pastels and Markal Paintstiks. Once again, the colour sits on the peaks and avoids the valleys, but with this method of application it is easy to create a broad and consistently even mark in seconds. With this technique we are aiming to highlight the raised areas of the quilting, not totally obliterate all detail. To this end, it is important to achieve a balance between the amount of paint and the pressure of the roller. We always sample on a scrap of quilted fabric first.

fabric focus Although most quilters use smooth fabrics for their wholecloth quilting, patchwork or appliqué, texture in the finished work is created by the tension of the quilt stitches, especially if there are lots of them closely spaced. Old quilts, washed so that the natural fibres of the wadding have shrunk in relation to the cotton fabrics that sandwich them, become beautifully dimpled. This antique look can be achieved easily by using a cotton wadding that is known to shrink the first time it is washed. Before making the quilt, the fabrics of the quilt top and back are prewashed but the wadding is not. Once the quilting is complete, the quilt is washed, allowing the wadding to shrink and the characteristic dimpling to occur. Hand-stitched embroidery and additional embellishments such as buttons, Shisha mirrors or beads can also be used to add a wonderful textural quality.

White acrylic paint is rolled gently across the hand-quilted surface with a paint roller made of soft sponge.

TIP Any paint left on the roller can be used on pages of a sketchbook, either as a band of pure colour or applied over a mask to create shapes.

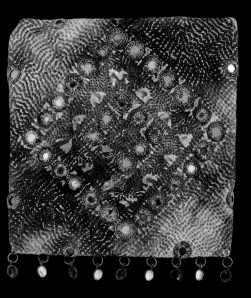

The little silk purse shown here, front (left) and back (right), features a panel of Shisha mirror work surrounded by very closely spaced quilting using hand-dyed embroidery thread. The quilted square was trimmed and bound before a final layer of white acrylic paint was gently applied. Once dry, the square was folded and invisibly stitched into an envelope shape and the bottom edge was embellished with beads.

Spraying

Spraying within a masked area is an excellent way to apply a fine and delicate mist of colour. Here we have created a frame by masking areas of a dyed and quilted surface with sheets of newspaper held in place with masking tape. Within the frame we have placed a freezer paper mask in the shape of a feather. We pinned the quilt to a wall so that it was easy to spray across the surface using an aerosol can of black fabric paint. It is easier to avoid accidental drips if the fabric is vertical rather than on a table or the floor. We applied the paint very sparingly at first, judging the effect and building up the density of colour gradually. Spraying from a very low angle accentuates the loft of the quilting and can create an almost 3-D effect.

Bird shapes sprayed on to a sketchbook page.

A stencil cut from a photocopy was used here with black spray paint and hand-dyed fabric.

TIP Layering two secondary colours such as orange with green or purple with green or all three primary colours (red, blue and yellow) will produce some variation of grey or brown, as may spraying a single colour on to an already coloured fabric. Choose colours of paint and fabric carefully to produce predictable results and, if in doubt, make a trial sample on paper or a scrap of fabric first.

fabric focus Most fabric paints are fixed by ironing. Obviously this is not as straightforward on a quilted item as on a single layer of cloth. Just press as carefully as possible to set the colour without completely flattening the quilting.

Sprayed colour around a feather-shaped mask, within a frame of masking tape.

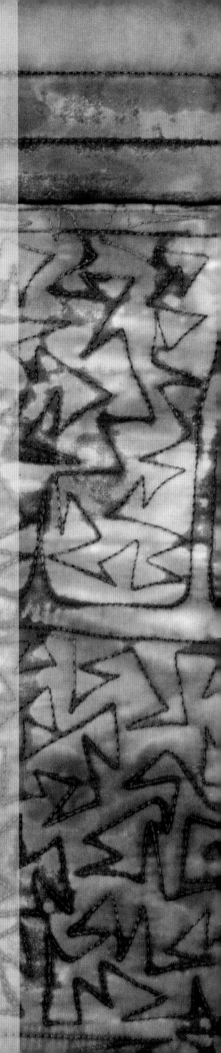

Removing Colour

Sometimes it can be just as exciting to remove colour from a fabric as it is to apply it! The most striking effects are achieved by starting with dark coloured fabrics because, once again, contrast is an important design principle with this technique. Charcoal grey is a personal favourite of ours and always seems to work well. The areas of discharged colour have a different quality to any other surface design technique, appearing almost luminous. Once bleached, the pale areas provide a perfect spot to introduce new colour, add a printed motif or maybe an appliqué.

Bleach or Discharge Paste

Pears discharged from Procion-dyed fabric.

Household bleach can remove colour from a range of watersoluble paints and inks, creating visually exciting sketchbook pages. It is one of our favourite techniques and you can see examples of how we use it in Chapter 2. Bleach dissolves the protein fibres of animal hair in artists' paintbrushes; we find sponge wedges, shapes cut from compressed craft sponge, wooden print blocks, scraps of card or cotton buds work well instead. We sometimes create sketchbook pages that we like so much we want to achieve a similar appearance on fabric. Many commercially printed, natural fibres and all cotton and linen fabrics that have been hand-dyed using fibre-reactive Procion MX dyes can be discharged to remove colour. The best results are achieved on dark coloured fabrics where discharged areas will have maximum value contrast with the original colour, as in the pears above. We often use bleach, but some people are concerned about the long term effects on the fabric and instead use a proprietary discharging agent. Jacquard Discharge Paste is a milky white paste that can be applied to fabric with a brush, sponge or by screen printing. The paste is allowed to dry completely, becoming virtually invisible until the heat of a steam iron discharges the dye to reveal the shape almost magically.

Previous page: *Reflections of a Shadow*, **detail, by Laura.**

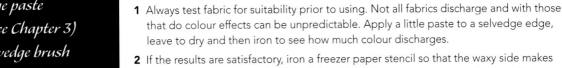

What you need

- *Discharge paste*
- *Fabric (see Chapter 3)*
- *Sponge wedge brush*
- *Firm sponge roller*
- *Paper stencil (those made from freezer paper are easiest to use)*
- *Iron*

1 Always test fabric for suitability prior to using. Not all fabrics discharge and with those that do colour effects can be unpredictable. Apply a little paste to a selvedge edge, leave to dry and then iron to see how much colour discharges.

2 If the results are satisfactory, iron a freezer paper stencil so that the waxy side makes contact with the right side of the fabric. Using freezer paper means the stencil won't move during the discharge process. It peels away easily and leaves no gluey residue on the fabric. If you don't have freezer paper, use a plain paper stencil, holding it carefully with one hand as you apply the paste. Alternatively, secure the stencil to the fabric with temporary spray adhesive.

3 Apply a thin layer of the discharge paste across the stencil aperture with a sponge wedge brush or roller (**a**).

Applying discharge paste through a photocopy cut as a stencil.

Ironing dry paste to remove colour.

4 Let the paste dry, remove the stencil and iron the cloth until the pale shape reveals itself (**b**). This should always be carried out in a well ventilated space. Discharged areas will become pale enough to have contrasting colour or fine detail introduced back into the shape using fabric paints or pigment markers.

The holes in compressed craft sponge contribute an interesting visual texture to bleach and discharge paste prints, as shown in this discharge print on black linen.

TIP For print applications using household bleach, a thicker product is easier to control. Proprietary bleach thickener makes a paste that remains stable for 24–36 hours.

Bleach Pens

Sometimes we might want to bleach narrow lines, include text or add other small detail to a quilt. It makes an interesting change to create these details by removing colour instead of the more usual additive techniques. Small shapes and fine lines of colour can be removed from Procion-dyed fabrics using bleach pens. These are sold in North America as a laundry product and for whitening tile grout rather than for art's sake (you decide if you'd rather be cleaning the bathroom, or working on a quilt!). The pens have two ends, one narrow and the other broader, each making a different type of mark when used on dyed fabrics.

Bleach begins to act on the colour of the fabric almost immediately and continues to spread across the cloth as long as it is wet. To achieve the narrowest lines, we rinse the fabric in lots of clean water as soon as the bleach mark is visible. If we are working on large items, this might mean we have to work on a small area at a time, stop the action of the bleach by washing, dry the fabric and, finally, continue the design. Tedious, but worth it for effects that look very different to those from any other surface design technique.

Sampling the marks made by the different ends, thick and thin, of a bleach pen.

A refillable plastic calligraphy pen.

materials focus If you can't find bleach pens and are impatient to try drawing with bleach, you could decant thick household bleach into a small plastic bottle that has a nozzle tip, or a calligraphy brush bottle that has a refillable reservoir. The finer the nozzle or brush, the narrower the mark you will be able to make. Avoid metal parts as they will corrode.

In this detail of *No One Knows*, the text was bleached with a pen after quilting.

Removing Colour After Quilting

As well as using discharge paste on fabric prior to quilting, it can also be added afterwards for a quite different effect. If the paste is applied to a densely quilted textile with the gentle pressure of a roller or sponge wedge brush, it will sit only on the raised areas of the surface. This means that the colour of the quilting stitch remains unchanged, as does a narrow halo area around each line of stitch. The raised, unquilted areas of fabric will, in contrast, lose their original colour and become pale when the dry paste is ironed. Ripples and wrinkles in the quilted fabric are enhanced and emphasized by the discharge process.

It is important to consider the colour of the fabric and thread before the discharge paste is applied and to imagine what will happen afterwards. With a process like this, a sample is highly recommended before any project is undertaken. Fabrics can react in an unpredictable way, producing surprising colour effects. Such a lot of time has to be invested before the final discharge process can occur and it would be frustrating to discover the result was not pleasing.

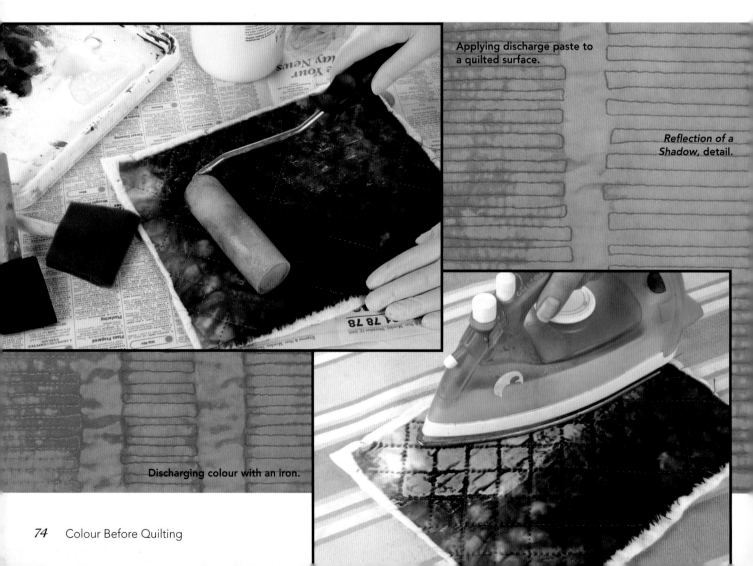

Applying discharge paste to a quilted surface.

Reflection of a Shadow, detail.

Discharging colour with an iron.

Replacing Discharged Colour

Surprisingly, by mixing Jacquard Discharge Paste with Jacquard Textile Paint in a single application, the colour that is discharged from the Procion-dyed fabric is magically replaced by the colour of the fabric paint. You can see how we have done this to introduce a pinky-red colour around the moth and into the background of the pear quilt. Both of these fabrics were essentially grey before the paste mixture was applied.

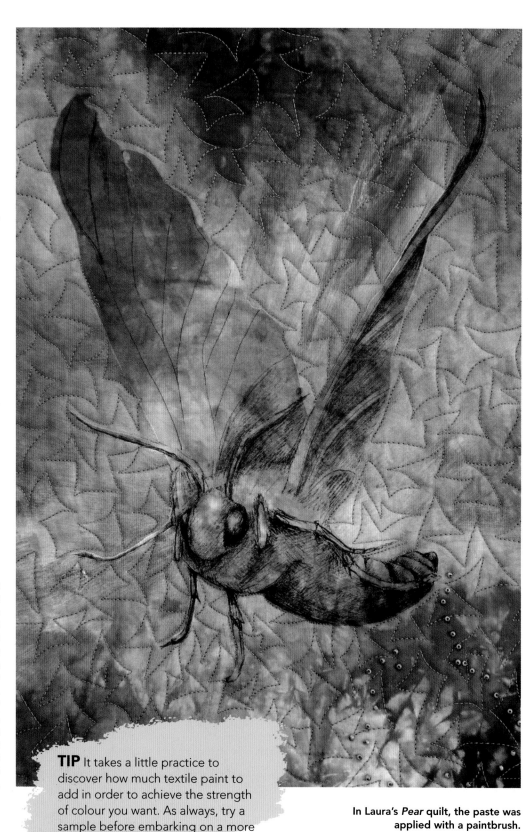

Here the paste and paint mix was applied over a paper mask with a sponge wedge brush. The brush was dragged off the edge of the paper shape so the thickness of the paste was greatest at the edge of the mask, decreasing the further away from the moth it travelled. This creates a halo of colour around the masked shape. Once the paste was dry, the fabric was ironed to remove the original dye colour and replace it with that of the paint. Details were added with a gel pen.

TIP It takes a little practice to discover how much textile paint to add in order to achieve the strength of colour you want. As always, try a sample before embarking on a more resolved piece.

In Laura's *Pear* quilt, the paste was applied with a paintbrush.

Adding
Detail

Often a painted quilt is broadly
realized by a technique or
combination of techniques that
produce the general effect but not
the fine detail that the quilt requires.
Depending on the choice of technique,
fine detail is usually added once the
general elements of the composition
are already in place. This could
happen before or after the quilting is
complete, but if detail is to be added
following the quilting, it is important
to leave a voided space that will
accommodate your intended design.

Painted Fusible Web

Double-sided fusibles such as Vilene's Bondaweb and Pellon's WunderUnder can be painted with diluted acrylic paint and, when dry, cut into shapes and ironed to transfer a layer of delicate colour to fabric. The transferred paint adheres to the cloth and, as long as the base fabric is suitable, items can later be gently hand-washed in cool water. Perlescent and metallic acrylic paints look wonderful on dark fabrics and can add a gorgeous richness to basic paint colours when transferred to any fabric. This colour transfer technique produces a fairly fragile surface suited to decorative items only. To increase resilience, secure the area of colour with stitch and/or a layer of transparent tulle.

Painted fusible shapes on pale and dark fabrics, showing the use of perlescent and metallic acrylic paints

Previous page: *Green Poppies* **by Laura, detail with sketchbook.**

What you need

- Double-sided fusible web such as Bondaweb or WunderUnder
- Diluted acrylic paint
- Fabric (see Chapter 3)
- Sponge wedge brush or large paintbrush
- Baking parchment
- Iron

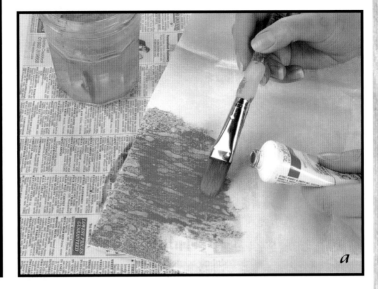

Applying dilute acrylic paint to fusible web.

1 To prepare the sheet of fusible, apply watery paint to the glue side with a sponge wedge brush or a large paintbrush (**a**). Make sure to paint the right side of the fusible! Paint the glue side, which feels rougher to the touch than the paper side. Be generous with the amount of water or the colour will be too opaque and heavy. As the glue layer becomes wet it partially lifts away from the paper backing creating lovely rippled patterns of texture.

2 When the paint has dried completely, cut out shapes (**b**), place them colour side down on to a smooth fabric and iron with a dry iron over baking parchment (**c**). Leave the shapes to cool for a few moments and then peel the paper backing away (**d**).

fabric focus The colour of the base fabric will show through areas of the transferred paint contributing to the effect. Consider how your choice of paint colours will appear in combination with that of the fabric.

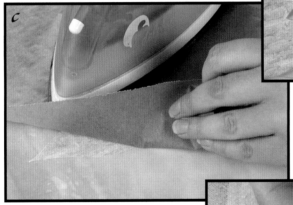

Shapes cut from painted fusible web.

Ironing the shape through baking parchment.

TIP Acrylic painted fusible will readily accept metallic transfer foils. Place a sheet of transfer foil, colour side facing up, over the painted shape, protect with a sheet of baking parchment and iron very gently with a medium heat setting. Ironing with too much pressure will mean the foil completely obliterates the paint rather than adding a subtle metallic gleam.

Removing the paper backing from the fusible web to reveal the transferred colour.

Gel and Other Fabric Pens

Fine lines, shading and pattern details can be added to fabric surfaces using permanent gel markers and pens. These products are made by many different manufacturers, but the brand is less important than the colour and nib size. It is useful to have a selection of pens – a fine nib for delicate lines, a medium nib for greater emphasis and a thick nib for really bold marks or if you need to ink in larger areas. Check the packaging to make sure that the ink is suitable for fabrics, and that it is permanent and washfast.

Laura's quilt, *David*, showing pen drawing.

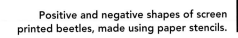

Positive and negative shapes of screen
printed beetles, made using paper stencils.

Much of the detail in Laura's quilt, *David* (opposite) was drawn direct to the hand-dyed cotton fabric just as if it were a sheet of paper. But don't worry if you aren't confident to draw freehand, or want a little help at the start of the drawing. On pale fabrics it is often possible to trace a pencil outline by placing the fabric over a photograph or line drawing of the subject. A lightbox makes it easier to see the basic outline especially when working with pale fabric. The tracing will probably be covered completely with the subsequent pen drawing but any pencil marks remaining visible after the pen drawing is complete can be removed with a fabric eraser.

Prints made using stencils make an ideal basis for adding detail with pens, as shown in these beetle prints; this masking technique produces a bold but simple positive or negative shape (above). The resulting prints allow plenty of scope for fine detail to be drawn in later with a black fabric pen (below).

Use pens to add patterns of dots, dashes or lines within the aperture of a stencil. Make closely spaced straight lines against a rule. Peel the stencil away to reveal a shape of pattern with a clearly defined edge.

TIP If you don't have a lightbox, try taping the line drawing and fabric to a bright, sunny windowpane.

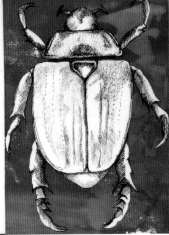

creative focus Look closely at your source of inspiration to inform and influence the details that you will include in the drawing. Are the marks thick, thin, continuous or broken? What direction do they follow? Are they straight or curved? Do they follow the contours of the subject? Think of the marks the pen makes just the same as if you were drawing with a pencil on paper. Closely spaced, curved lines will suggest a rounded form. Making all the marks go the same way lead the viewer's eye and create direction in a composition. Carefully placed areas of crosshatching make interesting shadows and create the illusion of 3D. Having lines converge at a point on the horizon suggests perspective and depth.

Beetle screen print with pen details.

Dimensional Paints

In Chapter 5 we talked a little about acrylic and fabric paints and the way they can be used after quilting. As well as these basic paints there are lots of other special effects products that are more suited to adding fine detail to quilts. Among our favourites are the various types of dimensional paints, which provide both colour and a 3-D surface.

Dimensional line paints are packaged in small plastic bottles and extruded through a fine nozzle tip. The paint can be used to make continuous lines or dots and dashes of colour. Used as directed by the manufacturers, the paint remains sitting on the surface of the fabric as a shiny, raised line when it is dry. Puff paints are applied in a similar way but swell on contact with the heat of an iron, applied when the paint is dry. These have a dull, almost rubber-like surface. Glitter paints, as the name suggests, contain metallic flakes suspended in a clear or coloured solution, especially effective on dark-coloured fabric where the glitter is easily seen.

Applying 3-D paint

Conventionally, all these products are applied by extruding the paint through the nozzle of the bottle so that a raised line of colour is produced. There are no rules to say it has to be that way! For drawing fine details, but where we don't want a line in relief, we place the tip of the bottle direct to the surface of the cloth and scribble as if we were sketching a mark on paper. It helps to tape the fabric to the work surface with short lengths of masking tape at each corner to prevent it from moving as you work. As we scribble, the point of the bottle tip scratches through the line of paint, producing a mark with an interesting and graphic quality. Because the paint surface is scratchy and irregular, the line dries flatter and with a much less obvious shine.

Sometimes we want to have a line with a completely flat appearance so we squeeze a little paint on to a palette and apply it to the fabric with a fine paintbrush. If we want to create a clearly defined shape, we might use a stencil and apply the paint from a palette using a sponge wedge brush.

TIP It is preferable to use special effects paints at the very final stage of making a quilt as they produce surfaces that are often difficult to stitch through.

A selection of dimensional fabric paints.

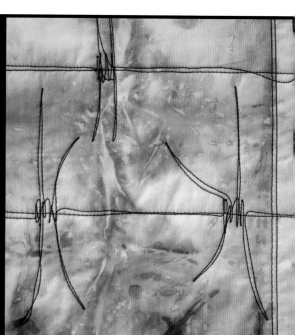

Quilting used to 'draw' lines of barbed wire.

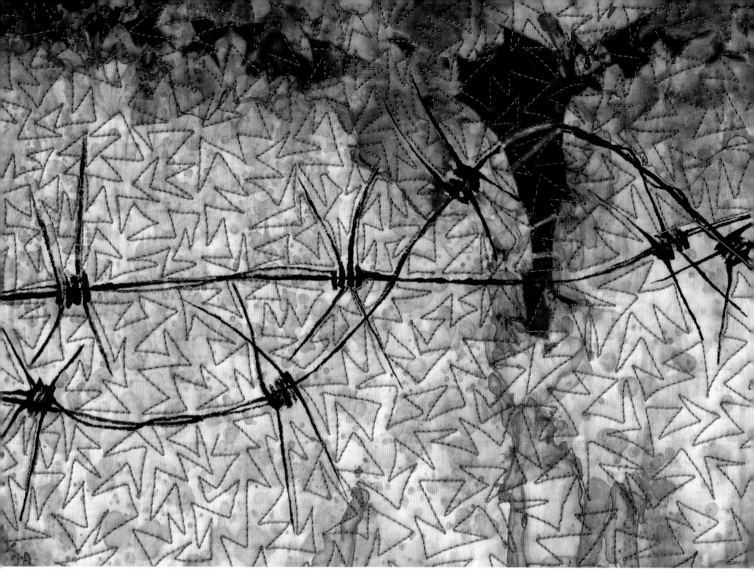

Laura's quilt, *Barbed Wire*, illustrates perfectly how effective it can be to draw direct to the surface of a quilt, especially when the intention is to produce narrow, linear marks. The shiny quality of the 3-D line paint seems appropriate for a metal subject such as barbed wire.

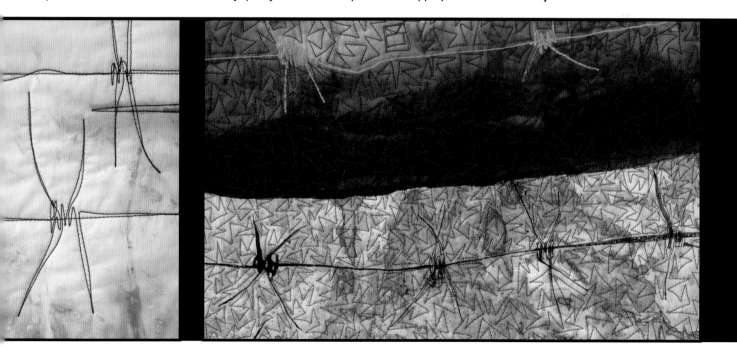

Pale colours of opaque paint show up on dark fabrics.

Adding text

Permanent marker pens are perfect for adding text to a quilt design. Make sure the pen you choose is waterproof and the ink lightfast. How is your handwriting? If it can bear close scrutiny, just make the words as though you were writing on paper and make sure you spell correctly! Curvy lines of text can be made to fit into a quilted shape, creating direction in a design. Words and phrases can be stretched or compressed to form more interesting shapes. The usual design principles apply so, if you want the message to stand out from the background fabric, consider the size of the script carefully and use a high contrast colour or value. For a more low-key appearance, make the letters smaller and use a pen with ink that is just two or three shades darker than the colour of the fabric you are writing on.

creative focus Rather than working freehand with a pen, you may prefer to use a stencil for more control over the shapes of the letters. The text on *David* (right) was made by printing the chosen computer font directly on to a sheet of freezer paper cut to fit an ink-jet printer. Each letter was cut out of the printed paper carefully with a scalpel to make a stencil that could be ironed to the fabric. (If you cut really carefully you can use both the positive and the negative shapes for different effects.) Markal pastel colour was applied through the holes of the stencil with an old toothbrush and then rubbed further into the fibres of the fabric with a fingertip.

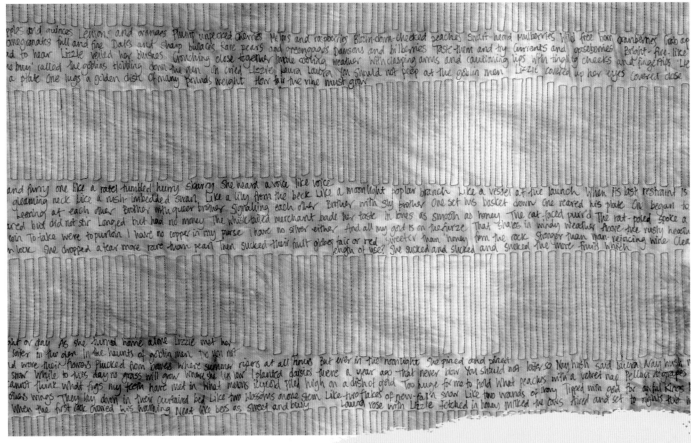

Laura's quilt, *Morning and Evening*, detail showing hand-written verse.

TIP Printing on to double-sided fusible web (see *Talisman*, right) can be a way of transferring all kinds of images, not just text. Bear in mind that ink-jet inks are not permanent on fabric without special treatment and so these transfers could not be washed!

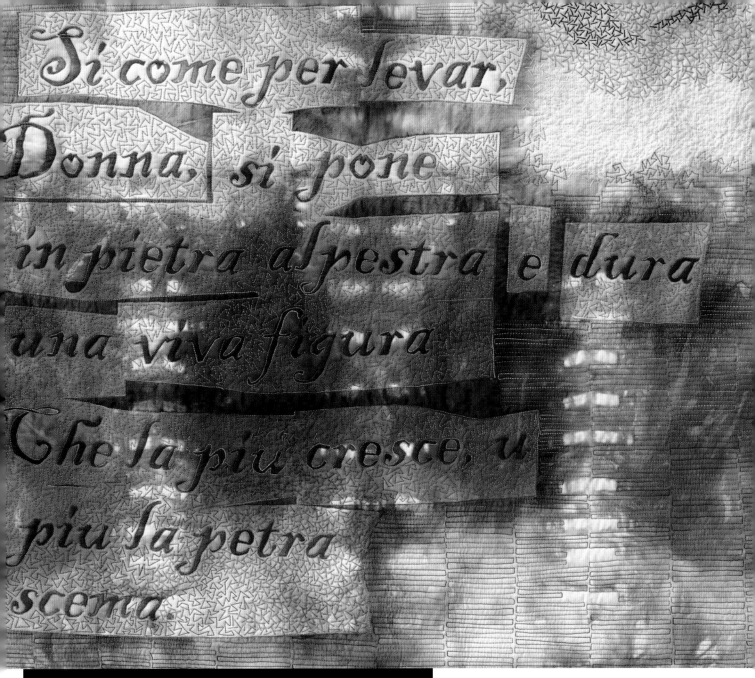

Sì come per levar,

Donna, sì pone

in pietra alpestra e dura

una viva figura

Che la più cresce, u

più la petra

scema

David detail showing text stencilled with Markal Paintstiks.

Talisman, detail showing text using printed fusible web. The text involved typing the words on the computer, flipping the image in a paint program to reverse the letters and printing on to the glue side of double-sided fusible interfacing, cut to fit the printer. Most home printers will accept a range of different paper-backed materials as long as they are not thicker than conventional print paper and the top edge is cut perfectly straight. The printed words were trimmed to remove excess unprinted background areas of the fusible web (which can look very shiny, especially on dark fabrics) and ironed to the quilt top. The paper was finally peeled away to reveal the text, now reverted to read the right way. There is a slight tackiness evident on the surface of the fusible webbing with this technique but it does disappear in a short time. The quality of the print is soft and broken rather than solid because of the open texture of the glue layer.

Pictorial and Figurative Images

It's because of a love of drawing and painting in general that we both enjoy creating pictorial compositions, especially those involving figurative subjects. We look to all kinds of painters for inspiration. Our tastes are eclectic, embracing the exquisite drawings and paintings of the Italian Renaissance, atmospheric domestic interiors, still life and pastoral images of Dutch 17th century artists, together with the less accessible Symbolist art of the 19th century.

Of course, there is a fine line between a painting providing inspiration for a quilt or simply becoming a copy – an interpretation in fabric and stitch! We try to strike a balance where the original source of inspiration remains evident but with our own personal contribution injected too.

Ink-jet Printing

Previous page: *Rose* by Linda.

One of the easiest ways to create images on fabric is with photo transfer paper produced for use in home printers. A sheet of photo transfer paper is placed in the printer so that the image prints on to the side that has a special coating. The ink is allowed to dry for a few minutes and the image trimmed to remove unwanted background areas. Finally, the printed image is placed on to the fabric and ironed as instructed by the product manufacturer.

A detail from the back of Laura's quilt, *Frances*, showing computer-enhanced images transferred to hand-dyed and bleached fabric.

There are two main types of heat transfer paper available; they are both commonly described as T-shirt transfer paper but the method of application is different for each and it is vital to know which you are using. One type of paper is used with the printed image face down to the fabric and ironed to transfer the image before the paper backing is peeled away. This is probably the most familiar product. The second type has appeared more recently but is now widely available. This has the paper backing removed after printing but before ironing the image to the cloth, with the printed image facing towards the iron. This, of course, means that there is no need to mirror image words and pictures on the computer before printing to enable them to 'read' correctly when transferred, as is necessary with the first product.

Although products do vary, all photo transfer paper does change the hand of the fabric considerably, leaving a plastic-like coating

that is not ideal for hand stitching. For this reason, it is a good idea to make the transfer print quite small so that no quilting is needed within the area of the image itself and all stitching can be placed at the edges of the print and beyond. We have found that the second type of paper (backing removed before transferring the image) produces a thinner, softer film and alters the hand of the fabric much less.

Treating fabrics for ink-jet printing

To make thin cotton and silk fabrics suitable for ink-jet printing, immerse them in a solution of Bubble Jet Set (see page 120 for suppliers), allow to dry over a shallow container and then iron. Back the fabric with freezer paper and cut carefully to the exact size to fit your printer. The paper backing will facilitate take-up of the fabric and help ensure a smooth feed through the machine. It is easily removed after printing and leaves no residue on the fabric. Leave the print to sit for 30 minutes then wash with cool water and a gentle detergent. The Bubble Jet Set solution makes the image permanent and washable without altering the hand of the fabric at all. The solution caught as the fabric drips dry can be reused.

Digital photograph printed on to fabric treated with Bubble Jet Set.

TIP These products are quite expensive. For the most economic use of transfer paper, aim to fill the entire sheet with printable images. If a single image doesn't fill the sheet by itself, position additional small images and cut them out to print individually.

fabric focus Very conveniently, various suppliers now stock packs of pretreated fabric sheets that can be used with most home printers. It is now possible to buy cotton, linen, sheer voile, organza and silk. Details of suppliers can be found on page 120.

Linda's cushion with photograph of honesty seedheads printed on fabric treated with Bubble Jet Set. The detail (right) shows the additional fabric painting and stitch used to integrate the print into the surrounding fabrics.

Photocopy Transfers

Photocopies, made on the kind of copy machines that use toner, can be transferred to the pages of a sketchbook or to fabric with cellulose (automotive) paint thinners. The photocopy is placed face down on to the surface to be printed, a little thinner is applied to a small area of the back of the paper with a brush and the now wet area is burnished using a metal lid from a jam jar. Use the flat top of the lid and press down with your fingers to make firm contact with the surface of the paper. Gradually the toner is dissolved and transfers across to the new surface below. Once this occurs, more solvent is applied to the adjacent area of the paper and the procedure continued until the whole image is completely transferred. If the transfer lacks definition and clarity, work into it, adding detail by drawing with a permanent pen to accentuate certain areas.

TIP Solvent transfers can be unpredictable. It is important to keep the photocopy paper and the fabric as still as possible as the transfer is made or the image will be blurred.

Detail from Laura's quilt, *Reflections of a Shadow*.

materials focus

Cellulose paint thinners are extremely unpleasant products in a confined space as the fumes are very strong. They should only be used with great caution, protective gloves and a suitable face mask. We always recommend working out of doors if possible. Bear in mind that you must never use plastic tools or containers with cellulose thinners.

Detail of Laura's quilt, *Frances*. The face was an ink-jet print, printed to fabric pretreated with Bubble Jet Set. Fabric paints were used to add further colour and shape.

Fabric Painting

Fabric painting is the perfect technique for creating large-scale pictorial compositions. It is also the easiest way to add extra colour to specific areas of a pastel rubbing or a stencilled motif. Because fabric paint sits on the surface of the cloth, it can be used on a wider range of fabrics, both natural and synthetic, than dyes, which are specific to a particular fibre content. Note that fabric paints may stiffen the hand of the cloth whilst dyes won't.

Fabric paints
There are lots of different fabric paints on the market. You may have to try several to find a favourite. The brand is probably less important than the colour and consistency so it is important to sample a product before planning a project. The fabric itself is also an important part of the equation as some fabrics are more absorbent than others. On fine or shiny fabrics, paints are more likely to spread than they are on thicker cloth, so it is important to sample the paint on the exact fabric intended for use in each project. To achieve crisp lines and fine detail when painting, the thickness of the paint and the absorbency of the cloth have to be balanced. Although a thin fabric might be the first choice for hand-quilting, it may also mean the paint flows too readily, making narrow lines and clearly defined edges difficult or impossible to achieve. Most fabric paints are fixed by ironing.

fabric focus Paint will automatically flow on wet fabric and, as long as there isn't too much liquid for the fabric to absorb, it tends to stop flowing when it reaches a dry area.

Detail of painted lemons from Linda's quilt, *The Fifth Day*.

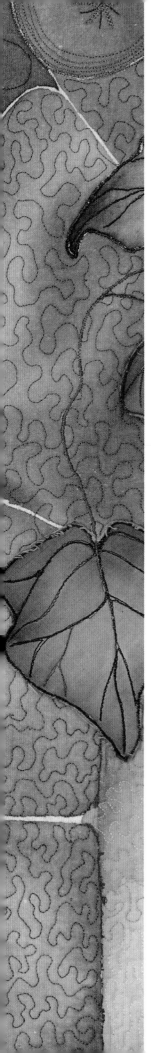

Detail of painted dragonflies and angel's face in *The Fifth Day*.

Detail of feathers from the angel's robe and fish in *The Fifth Day*. This quilt, shown in its entirety on page 9, was inspired by the stained glass designs of Edward Burne-Jones. It was painted with dilute fabric paints to create an effect similar to that of a watercolour painting. A faint pencil line was first sketched on to the cloth as a guide for the painting. (For anyone not confident to draw freehand, it could have been traced from an image using a lightbox.) The paint was applied to dry cloth where a hard edge was required and, where the colour needed to spread more, the area was first wet with a brush dipped in clean water.

Acrylic Paint

Because we always have it on hand and because there are so many gorgeous colours, we often prefer to use acrylic paint instead of a paint made specifically for fabrics. Most manufacturers of acrylic paint also offer a compatible fabric medium, which, when mixed with the paint, makes it more flexible and the painted fabric remains a little softer than if it is used without. Although it can be washed with care, we wouldn't normally recommend acrylic paint for use on quilts made for beds, but for items that don't require regular laundering, for instance box lids, mirror frames or anything that will be displayed on a wall, it is fine. Once dry, acrylic paint requires no fixing.

Painting with Procion MX as a dye paste

When we want to paint fabric but maintain the softness of natural cotton, linen or silk fibres, we might choose to use thickened Procion dye rather than acrylic paint or fabric paint. Using the same basic dyes, but in a thicker format, also means the colours of our hand-dyed fabrics will perfectly complement those that we paint. Procion used as a paste means we can control how far dyes will spread and allows us to achieve distinct colour separation in a painting.

We thicken the dye with sodium alginate (see pages 38–39 for paint paste recipe). Thickened dye can be applied with a palette knife or a brush or, if made slightly thinner, it can be decanted into plastic bottles and squirted out through a nozzle tip. This isn't an exact science! It is necessary to experiment with the thickness of the paste balanced with the size of the hole in the bottle cap to achieve predictable results. Squirting paste through a nozzle makes linear designs and text very easy – just like using a pen to write and draw. Thickening the dye means the applied colour stays where it is put. It holds every brush or palette knife mark where it has been placed on the cloth and the paste inhibits further spread of the dye.

fabric focus Remember that, like all dye applications, the thickened colour will only fix to soda-treated fabric and has to be kept moist by covering with plastic until that reaction has occurred. If you are working on a large piece, be aware of the risk of some areas drying out before the rest of the fabric is painted. You may have to spray with a fine mist of water to keep the dye moist until you can cover it with a sheet of plastic.

The head of Circe poisoning the sea in Linda's quilt, *Circe's Spell,* has been painted using artists' quality acrylic paint mixed approximately half and half with fabric medium. A little extra water was added to encourage the flow of the paint in places where the colour needed to be gently blended. Harder edges of colour were produced with thicker paint and a drier brush. The general outlines of the facial features were first drawn in pencil on to white cotton fabric. The painting of these areas was carried out using a fine sable paintbrush. Only Titanium White, Naples Yellow, Ultramarine Blue and Cadmium Red paint were used to mix all the flesh colours, shadows and hair colour. In addition, Paynes Grey was added for dark details in and around the eyes. For the finished quilt, see pages 118–119.

In this painted pear design, the marks of the palette knife are very evident, adding visual texture and interest to the fabric surface.

materials focus Because the paste is thicker than ordinary dye it may appear slightly raised on the surface of the fabric. Only the dye that is actually in contact with the fibres can react and fix, so it is normal to see a substantial amount of excess colour wash away when dye painted fabric is rinsed. To minimize this waste, aim to apply the colour as thinly as possible.

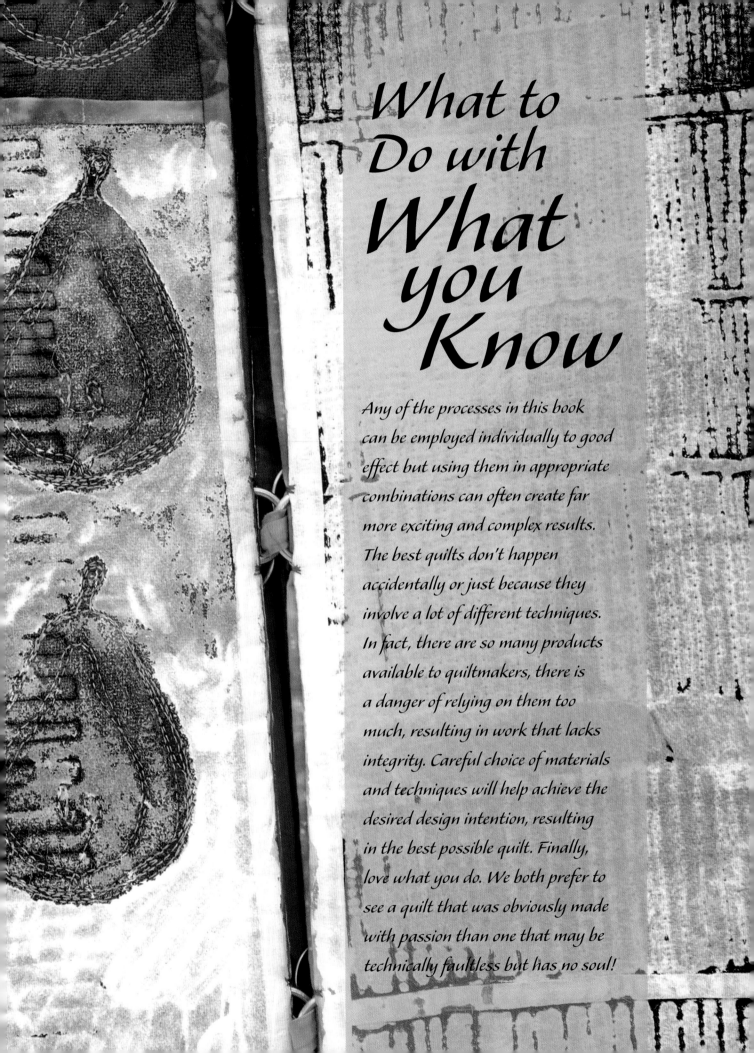

What to Do with What you Know

Any of the processes in this book can be employed individually to good effect but using them in appropriate combinations can often create far more exciting and complex results. The best quilts don't happen accidentally or just because they involve a lot of different techniques. In fact, there are so many products available to quiltmakers, there is a danger of relying on them too much, resulting in work that lacks integrity. Careful choice of materials and techniques will help achieve the desired design intention, resulting in the best possible quilt. Finally, love what you do. We both prefer to see a quilt that was obviously made with passion than one that may be technically faultless but has no soul!

What is a Quilt?

In a book dedicated to the painted quilt it is appropriate to pose the questions, 'what is a quilt and what exactly are quilts for?' The answer is they are whatever you want them to be! The qualification to that is they must be fit for purpose, whatever that purpose might be. Many quilts are purely for display but if they are made for a bed, they must withstand daily wear and tear. Some of the techniques we use are fairly robust while others are more suited to quilts as decoration, or for a variety of quilted items such as vessels and boxes, rather than as functional, everyday coverings for beds. Although the products we use are sold as permanent for use on cloth, some of the surfaces we create are too fragile to withstand the regular washing that a bed quilt demands, especially a child's quilt. You must decide what will suit your own project.

Sketchbook pages showing Laura's studies of hedgerows using dye and charcoal (left) and drawings with charcoal and eraser (right).

Quilts as art

I began making quilts more than 30 years ago and followed a conventional path; consequently I have enough bed quilts to last several lifetimes. Laura, now in her twenties, obviously came to quiltmaking much more recently and she has bypassed quilts for beds entirely, choosing instead to express her design ideas in quilts for walls or as freestanding installations. We make our quilts for display and decoration, often using them in our homes as others might hang a painting. Quilts are often sidelined as domestic items rather than considered as art but we believe the work is as valid as any other creative genre. If there is a message in an art quilt, it doesn't have to be controversial or political, it is just as likely to be a personal observation of something we find fascinating in the world around us. There is certainly nothing wrong with creating designs for quilts just because we think they are beautiful.

The design process

What makes a quilt original in a world where there is nothing new under the sun? Originality in design is always in direct relation to the personal contribution of the maker. So where does anyone begin? Collecting images that grab the imagination, taking photographs of anything that catches the eye and developing the habit of drawing regularly in a sketchbook is a good start. Most artists are inspired by the world they see around them. A collection of visual information gradually grows into a valuable design resource that can be returned to again and again. When we want to work with a particular subject, the collection of images is the first place we look. We continue to add to the collection all the time and to make our own drawings and sketches from the photos too. This is a basic good practice that allows us to explore and develop any theme.

The process of designing and making is about asking oneself a series of simple questions. No one arrives at a fully formed idea for a finished design without establishing a few fundamental

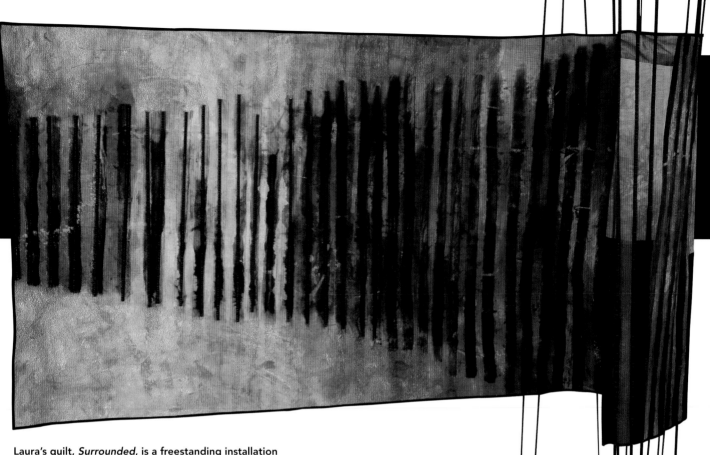

Laura's quilt, *Surrounded*, is a freestanding installation piece. 304cm x 91cm (120 x 36in) excluding the sticks.

facts beforehand. What are you making? Who are you making it for? How do you want it to look? The answers to those three questions will provide much of the information you need to get started. Designing an item with a specific function and site in mind is always the easiest way of working. The function determines the type of materials and techniques that will be suitable. The site probably dictates a maximum

size and appropriate proportions. Placing a quilt into an interior means that an existing colour scheme, architectural details and general decorative style have to be taken into account.

The following pages show a selection of our quilts, made using techniques described previously in this book. Some of them I made myself, some are by Laura and others were projects we worked on together.

Reflections of a Shadow and Feels Like Home *(Laura)*

Laura is using form more and more in her own quilts. Much of her recent work has involved installation pieces designed to be free standing rather than for display on a wall. These pieces, often figurative, are designed to engage the attention of the audience. To this end, the viewer is encouraged to interact with the works by walking around and between them, making their eye level the same as that of the figures in the quilts. Laura works through her ideas very fully in her sketchbooks long before she even thinks of fabric and stitch. The books that she gradually fills with colour, line and shape are an integral part of the design process for her and, although they usually lead her on to textile work, they could be viewed as fully resolved and complete works in their own right.

creative focus To achieve a visual relationship from one 'page' to the next of a book quilt, or across a series of panels designed to hang closely together, it is a good idea to involve some common element. Continuity can be achieved by taking a colour, line or shape around to the other side of the 'page' or across the gap between two panels. In Laura's *Reflections of a Shadow*, a horizontal band of piecing or corresponding colour occurs towards the top third of every page.

Reflections of a Shadow **shown (from left to right) with 'pages' closed to the right, pages open, a different page, pages closed to the left. 164 x 124cm (65 x 49in).**

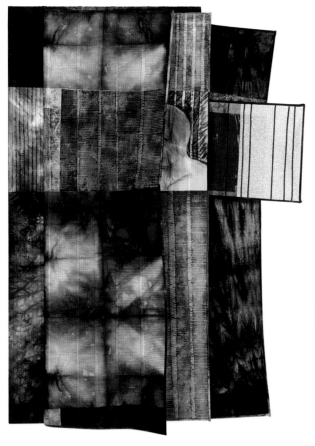

The quilt in book form

The important role her sketchbooks play has led Laura to consider the actual book form as a structure for a quilt. She had already explored the potential of generously sized flaps as seam insertions in her quilt, *Metamorphosis*, made in 2002 (see pages 40–41). Extending the narrow flaps to become larger 'pages' was a simple step. Insertions of 3-D panels into the seams of a 2-D surface allowed her a greater scope for narrative content. These are multi-faceted quilts that are either attached to the wall at the spine, or displayed flat on a plinth. The pages provide extra surface area for additional design elements and more variety of technique. Not all the faces of the quilt can be viewed simultaneously so that, as the pages are turned, the contents are revealed and the visual effect constantly changes.

Reflections of a Shadow is the largest 'book' quilt to date. The title came from a song lyric by David Crosby. The pages reveal glimpses of Laura's sister, Frances, transferred to the cloth with photocopy transfer techniques using cellulose (automotive) thinners. The fabrics have all been hand-dyed and/or screen-printed with subsequent applications of Markal Paintstiks. Finally, following quilting, the raised surfaces of the cloth were discharged by applying discharge paste with a soft sponge roller.

Laura's *Feels like Home* is a smaller version of the book format made to celebrate moving to a new house. The dusty looking surfaces of the quilted pages reflect the state of a house that requires some attention and not a little TLC. 55 x 44 x 39cm (21.5 x 17.5 x 15.5in).

"By combining appropriate techniques carefully and thoughtfully, it is possible to integrate a number of disparate elements without the composition looking disjointed."

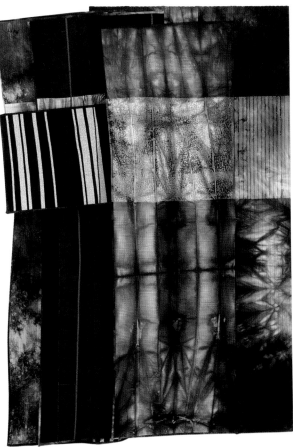

Signs, Symbols, Spirit *(Linda)*

Following a visit to the fascinating Pitt Rivers Museum in Oxford, England, I was intrigued by the incredible artefacts I saw in the dimly-lit interior of the building. There are cabinets and shelves packed with the strangest objects from all corners of the world: amulets, shrunken heads, talismans and curses, wrapped in cloth and sealed forever with wax and thorns. Tall chests with drawer after drawer reveal their surprising, sometimes shocking, contents to the inquisitive visitor. The African shields of wood, skin and fibre particularly held my imagination and as soon as I got home I felt inspired to draw, print and paint into a sketchbook. These sketchbook pages eventually led to three narrow quilts and three tall, mixed media towers.

I believe that it was the experience of the visit itself and the atmosphere of the actual building housing such an eccentric collection that provided the inspiration as much as the artefacts themselves. I never intended to be too literal with the source of inspiration but I did want to capture the essence of the original objects. The integrity of the raw materials was important. I loved their natural quality, sense of age and purpose. The features I focused on initially included the colours of the hide, wood and leather, the marks and patterns of decoration and the woven textures of some areas of the shields.

The actual colour palette of the shields was, for the most part, dark and dusty – animal skins, old wood and years of being handled had darkened the surfaces to a rich patina. I was intending to display my pieces in a contemporary setting and so decided to change the colours quite radically but to maintain the sense of dustiness and age. My chosen palette referred to elemental earth colours but used soft ochres and greys in place of the burnt sienna and red of the original design source.

Some of the shields were elongated ovals and some rectangular. I chose to use the elegant proportions of the rectangle for my overall shape but to include the oval shield shape as a motif within the design. These shield-like shapes were applied to the hand-dyed cotton fabrics as thickened Procion dye monoprints. This technique creates the same primitive appearance as the original surfaces and patterns of the shields and so was more suitable than other techniques. If, for instance, I had used appliqué, the edges of the shapes would have inevitably been more clearly defined – not the look I was aiming for at all.

"I never intended to be too literal with the source of inspiration but I did want to capture the essence of the original objects."

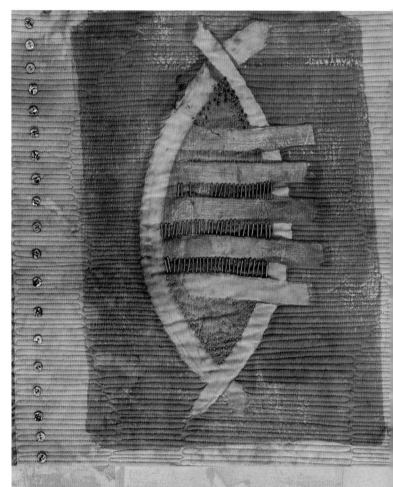

creative focus For *Spirit*, I used continuous free motion machine quilting to describe a basketweave pattern reminiscent of the woven fibres of some of the shields and added natural shell buttons inspired by the patterns of little dots I had noticed decorating the shields. Finally, I added beads and hand embroidery to create areas of crunchy texture. Crudely made cross-shaped marks were a common pattern on several of the shields. I was able to use simple stitches to represent these details.

Signs.
157 x 48cm
(62 x 19in).

Symbols.
143 x 47cm
(56.5 x 18.5in).

Spirit.
48 x 110cm
(19 x 43.5in).

Right:
Sketchbook pages
with collage,
monoprinting and
paint.

Below:
Sketchbook pages
with acrylic paint
monoprints.

Beetle Collection (Laura)

As we discussed in Chapter 4, screen printing is the perfect technique to choose when you need multiple images of the same subject. Laura has used two different sizes of paper stencil to print the rather scary beetles on her quilt, *Beetle Collection*. The composition of the quilt was inspired by the idea of Victorian butterfly, beetle and insect collections where the exhibits were arranged formally in rows, held by a metal pin through the thorax and displayed in shallow cabinets or drawers. Each beetle in the collection would be a perfect example of a single species and, although perhaps superficially similar to the next in the collection, would have some notable differences.

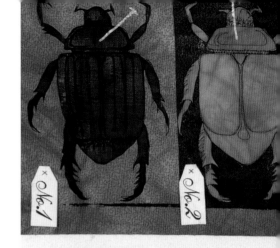

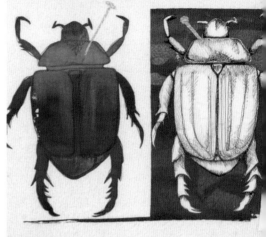

Beetle Collection. 144 x 79cm (57 x 31in).

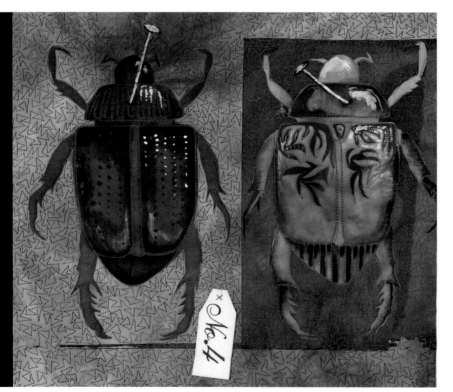

TIP Completely different colours of screen prints can be made to work together in a single quilt top. Identify a significant dye colour from one beetle and match it with either fabric paint or Markal Paintstik. Apply small accents of the colour to the adjacent beetle. You may need to do a reciprocal procedure, taking a colour from the second beetle back to the first. The colour of the quilting thread can do a similar thing, visually marrying the two separate prints by introducing a common element.

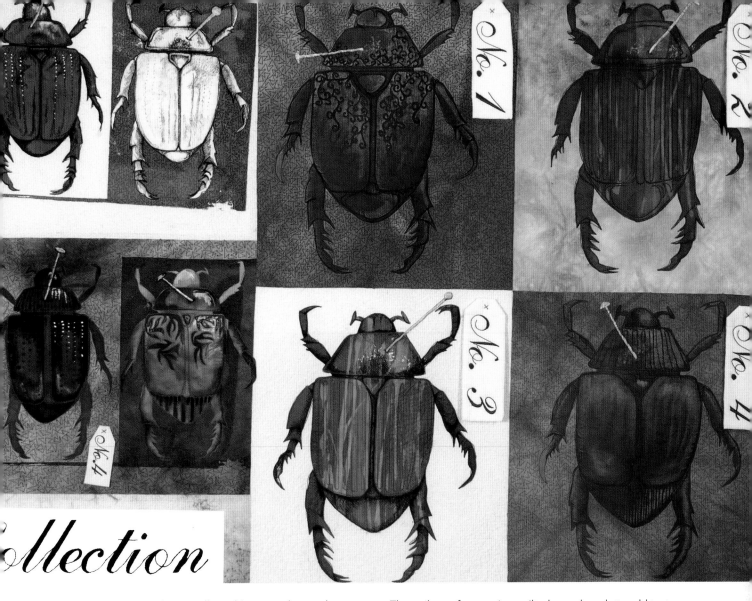

Collection

Using the screen printing technique allowed Laura to change the colour of the thickened dye each time a print was made, so that, like the beetles, each print is slightly different from the next. Adding the dye in separate and distinct areas of the screen resulted in natural looking stripes – perfectly convincing as the kind of colours you might well see on exotic beetle wing cases.

Because she used both the positive and negative shapes of the paper stencils, the resulting prints are produced as pairs with interchanged colour. The different characteristics of the prints are further emphasized with hand-drawn linear details using permanent marker pens as well as additional colour from fabric paint and Markal Paintstiks.

The quilt was free motion quilted very densely to add texture to the background and yet more detail, texture and pattern to the beetles. Finally, Markal was used again to add highlights to some of the beetles' backs and silver colour added to the pins with metallic fabric paint. The name of the quilt was embroidered by machine and pieced as part of the quilt top. Little stitched labels were attached to some of the prints in the same way that paper labels might have been used to describe the contents of the Victorian collection. These were also machine embroidered.

Laura worked the same print direct to her sketchbook page.

Fields of Gold
(Laura and Linda)

The quilts illustrated here are from a series of four, entitled *Fields of Gold*, which were created in response to the song lyric by Sting and made for a two-man exhibition of our work in France. We both took the same phrase and produced our own interpretations independently. Working with loud music playing in the background and listening to song lyrics is a constant source of inspiration. We accept that some people find music a distraction and have even read that if you do choose to listen to music it should only ever be instrumental because music with words interferes with the creative side of the brain! We can only speak for ourselves when we say that lyrics paint pictures in our heads and often provide titles for our quilts at the same time.

Nature also provided inspiration for these quilts. Living in the country, we are surrounded by fields that are drab and brown in winter, bright lime green in early spring and golden ochre in late summer and autumn. We see these fields through the windows as we work on our quilts and love the mellow colours of the tall grass when we have been lucky to have a long, hot summer. This is sheep country and often the grass is cropped and short but sometimes the farmer plants barley and the tall, graceful seedheads move with the wind like waves at sea.

Unusually for me, I bought most of the fabrics used in these pieces, including the mustard coloured fabric of the foreground with its irregular, vertical stripes. For my quilt, *Fields of Gold II*, I voided these as I free motion quilted with closely spaced horizontal lines. Leaving the narrow channels unquilted raised them relative to the background surface, creating the suggestion of stalks. I 'drew' the seedheads with lines of quilting as I stitched and went back in later to accentuate the shapes with gold and copper metallic fabric paints. Horizontal bands of fabric reinforce the simple illusion of landscape and an appliquéd sun, shadowed with a layer of black Markal, completes the composition.

Linda's quilt, *Fields of Gold II*, is the small, middle quilt of a series created in response to the song lyric by Sting and made for a joint exhibition. 50 x 143cm (20 x 56in).

creative focus Lines can be so subtle they are almost invisible or they can dominate a design. Consider the different visual impact of a line of straight stitches made by machine quilting with that of a broad line of satin stitch for instance, or the broken line of dashes formed by hand-quilted stitches. Colour and value contrast emphasizes the effect of any line – think how much more visible a line of satin stitch would be if the colour of the thread contrasted greatly with that of the fabric. A row of white satin stitch on white fabric introduces texture as much as line, while a row of black satin stitch on white fabric would be very dramatic.

Fields of Gold II, detail. Line is an important design element in this quilt. It features in the large expanse of foreground as both narrow vertical channels and as densely quilted columns.

Laura's *Fields of Gold* incorporates a screen print of the lyric made by writing the words in hot wax on the screen. Once dry, the wax acted as a resist as thickened dye was pulled across it with the squeegee, leaving white words on a coloured background on the printed fabric. The screen print was combined with other painted and monoprinted fabrics. Finally, Markal was applied to modify the colour in some areas before quilting by machine. 72 x 145cm (28.5 x 57in).

Pear Hanging *(Laura)*

This small hanging, which would be perfect on a dining room wall, involved multiple applications of a number of different techniques. It started life as wire rubbings made with Markal Paintstik on white cotton cloth. The rubbings were left to cure and then fixed by ironing. General colour was applied to the cloth by painting with Pebeo Setacolor transparent paints, adding a little water to help them flow more readily. Working with the fabric on top of a sheet of crumpled plastic meant that interesting hard-edged shapes appeared in the paint where it pooled in the creases. Laura used a large artist's paintbrush and made definite gestural marks with the paint to add even more visual texture. When dry, the fabric paint was fixed by ironing. At this point the hanging was free motion quilted to add texture and substance.

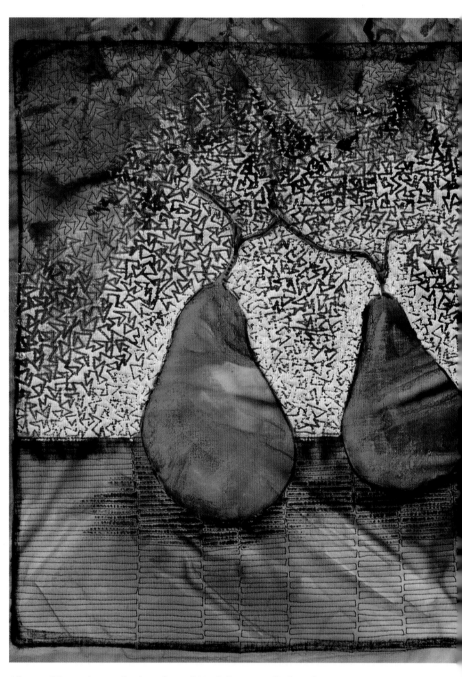

After quilting, a layer of pale-coloured Markal was applied to the top section to emphasize the contours of the two pears and accentuate the texture created by the quilting. Shadows, to suggest the fruit were resting on a table, were drawn in with a dark blue Markal. Finally, a line to frame the entire composition was created by rubbing over the edge of a cutting mat placed beneath the fabric.
64 x 50cm (25 x 19.5in).

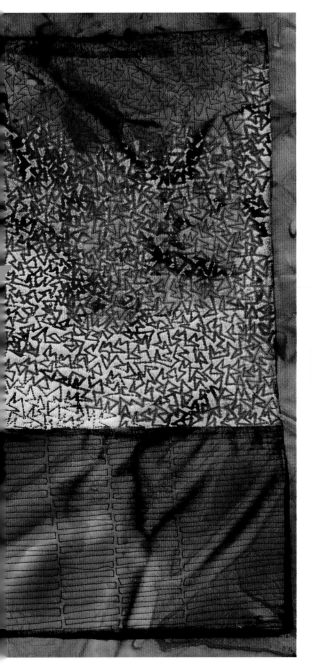

A page from Laura's sketchbook showing drawing and painting combined with text.

More from Laura's sketchbook, this time the text is a screen print made direct to the page.

Hydrangea Pillow *(Linda)*

Hydrangeas are a common flowering plant in English gardens and also immensely popular in France where many festivals honour them each summer. They are undeniably beautiful plants with incredibly subtle variations of colour and form. The huge flower heads appear to be very complex structures and, consequently, difficult to draw, but it is easy to take a single floret and build a design from that.

In Chapter 2 you saw pages from a sketchbook where we made use of stencils with soft pastels on painted paper and with oil pastels combined with a gently coloured watercolour wash. We have also talked about stencilling on fabric using the same hydrangea motif (pages 42–43). The fabric for this pillow was produced in just the same way as those earlier samples using an identical stencil.

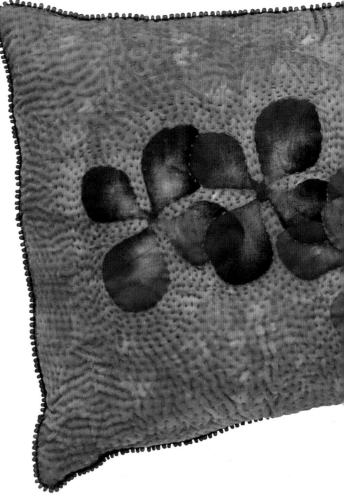

This detail shows how the cream coloured hydrangea florets were spaced with strings of glass beads and matching beads were stitched along the edges of the pillow as a final embellishment.

creative focus To make the tassels, the hydrangea floret was printed several times on to a sheet of heat transfer photo paper. That was ironed to a pale fabric and in turn bonded with double-sided, fusible interfacing (Bondaweb) to a blue fabric. Each shape was cut out carefully exactly at the edge of the petals. There was no need to worry about fraying as the transfer paper and the fusible webbing prevented this from being a problem.

TIP It's a good idea to include a few loosely wound skeins of thread whenever you dye a batch of fabrics. This ensures you will always have the perfect thread for future projects. Fairly fine, single strand cotton and silk is best for quilting.

Hand-quilted *Hydrangea Pillow*. Notice how tightly the threads of the quilting were pulled. By increasing the tension, the fabric is encouraged to pucker more than usual, making it beautifully textured. 46 x 23cm (18 x 9in).

Once the design arrangement and colours were decided upon in a sketchbook, I substituted Markal Paintstik for oil pastel and Procion dye took the place of the watercolour wash so that it was possible to achieve the same effects on fabric. The paper stencil was moved many times to produce multiple images of florets, each one slightly overlapping its neighbour. The colours used were deliberately limited to blue, green and turquoise. Because these transparent colours were applied to an indigo blue fabric, the results are very subtle, with little contrast between the background fabric colour and that of the floral motifs. Notice how different this makes the flowers appear when compared to the stronger, brighter colours that were used in the Hydrangea hanging on pages 42–43.

When the stencilling was complete, the Markal was allowed to cure, the colour fixed by ironing and finally the stencilled fabric was layered with batting and backing and basted to secure the sandwich. It was then hand-quilted with a single strand, variegated embroidery thread. I beaded the edges of the pillow by adding a single tiny glass seed bead to each blanket stitch. To finish off the pillow, I made a decorative tassel for one corner, using photo image transfers interspaced with the same blue/green beads as around the edges.

Sketchbook pages are an ideal place to record the colour, line, texture and shape of the design source.

Landscape Hangings *(Linda and Laura)*

Laura and I thought it would be interesting to make a series of simple landscape-inspired hangings and subject each of them to slightly different painting techniques to see how their basic appearance could be changed. Four tops were first strip-pieced using a limited colour palette influenced by a couple of magazine pictures, and the shapes and proportions were developed by referring to several small paper collages (see pages 22–23). The fabrics were mostly hand-dyed cottons but the occasional scraps of hand-dyed linen and wool also crept in. Involving contrasting textures of fabrics adds immediate interest to the quilt surface and also affects the appearance of subsequent applications of paint, print and stitch.

Hanging 1 **with bird and feathers.**
47 x 85cm (18.5 x 33.5in).

Hanging 2 **with black moon and barley. 47 x 76cm (18.5 x 30in).**

Hanging 1

Here the pieced top had a photographic image transfer of the moon ironed to it. Placing a recognizable object in the 'sky' made the compositions more convincing as landscapes. A bird, cut from black fabric, was bonded to the top section so that the outstretched wings made interesting shapes across the sky. These were used to suggest the pattern the quilting would take. To fill the rather large and empty foreground, a row of oversized feathers was added by cutting a freezer paper mask and stencilling with Markal Paintstiks. The quilting in this area was made to 'draw' detail within the feather shapes. By contrast, the surrounding areas were closely quilted in vertical columns of horizontal lines.

When the quilting was complete, dark acrylic paint was used on the bird appliqué to disguise the stitched edges and blend the colours of thread with the fabric a little more. Highlights of white acrylic were painted to the top of the head, the ridge of the beak and the scaly, bare legs. The eyes were accented with tiny lines of colour using a very fine paintbrush. This hanging was achromatic (without colour) at this point and too dull for the low-key composition, so touches of crimson pastel were added at the edges of the feathers. So that the crimson did not overwhelm the more subtle bird and moon elements, touches of pinky-red fabric were introduced to bind sections of the quilt. We also attached feather and bead embellishments at one side of the hanging (a bit of a nonsense but everyone should be allowed to be frivolous from time to time!).

Hanging 2

Although smaller, this looked fairly similar to *Hanging 1* at first. We quilted the whole piece by machine and then printed a sphere of black acrylic paint to represent the moon, using a circle of compressed sponge. Plain black looked rather flat so, when the paint was dry, we printed a second layer on top using a much paler colour. Free motion quilting was worked in the foreground to draw stalks of barley on top of the quilted surface. One of the barley seedheads was painted with gold fabric paint and a touch of the same colour smeared across the top of the moon.

Hanging 3

This was monoprinted with a sketchy drawing of a spiralling moon on the blue woollen fabric sky. The monoprint was made by rolling a smooth layer of black acrylic paint to a sheet of template plastic, quickly drawing marks into the wet paint and flipping the plastic over on to the patchwork. This is a rather unpredictable process and certainly deserves a trial run on paper first. The test piece helps determine the correct amount and wetness of paint, the suitable size of drawing and the pressure required to transfer the colour but, because the fabrics accept colour differently to paper, the actual print is, to a degree, in the lap of the gods! Dark, broad lines and thinner white lines were monoprinted in the foreground using a colour shaper tool to make marks in the acrylic paint. Ears and stalks of barley were embroidered by hand to add an accent of colour among the vertical printed lines.

Hanging 4

In this quilt we included the same photo transfer of the moon that was used in *Hanging 1*. The photo was taken in the 1880s and had a lovely quality to it, quite unlike modern photographs. A broad strip of the quilted foreground was made paler with Jacquard Discharge Paste and lots of tiny natural shell buttons were attached in rows. The shiny buttons suggest reflections and ask the question, 'Is this land or water?'

Hanging 3 with monoprinted moon and grasses. 32 x 43cm (12.5 x 17in).

materials focus

Mid grey thread was used throughout the quilting in *Hanging 1*. Using a single neutral colour unified the surface without the distraction that additional contrasting colours of thread would provide. It was amazing how the relative value of the grey thread seemed to change as it travelled across the fabrics. Seen against very dark, sombre fabrics, it looked a pale and bright silver. It completely disappeared when it was crossing mid grey fabrics and then reappeared as a really dark line on areas of pale grey.

Hanging 4 with black moon and shell buttons. 32 x 52cm (12.5 x 20.5in).

Black and White Feathers *(Laura)*

This quilt challenges lots of preconceptions about contemporary quiltmaking practice. It is a common belief that most people who have come to quilting in recent years, the age of the rotary cutter and template-free piecing, want instant gratification, quick fixes and an easy resolution. Those of us who have been making quilts for more years than we care to count have probably learnt our skills the traditional way. We have worked our way through all the old-fashioned patchwork techniques, made our own templates and probably once stitched everything by hand. New tools, equipment and quilting notions have made our patchwork much quicker and easier now. There is also an increasing acceptance of machine skills and the contribution they can make to the craft. Having said that, this quilt of Laura's, *Black and White Feathers,* is, in many ways, looking back to the established old traditions. It is a hand-quilted wholecloth, very conventionally worked in white thread on white cotton cloth. The design is also entirely traditional, involving running feathers, plaits and chains.

Where the design and construction departs from the conventional approach is that, following hundreds of hours of meticulous hand quilting, Laura recklessly and with abandon, painted across the stitched surface! The quilt had been quilted with quite a tight stitch tension so that the surface was dimpled with texture. The batting had not been prewashed. This was intentional because Laura wanted the shrinking to happen after quilting in order to achieve the same lovely texture that makes antique quilts feel so wonderfully tactile. She washed the quilt so that the cotton and alpaca batting would shrink, making the quilt even more textured and dimpled than it had been before.

After washing, she painted the area where she intended to place the figure with a thin covering of acrylic, matte gel medium. (This is not a quilt that will ever be washed – it is more a painting that happens to be on a quilted textile sandwich.) The layer of acrylic gel primes the surface and makes it more receptive to drawing and painting. The haunting and mysterious figure was drawn on to the primed surface spontaneously, using a combination of graphite pencil and dilute fabric paint. Deeper value was added with acrylic paint and Markal Paintstiks and fine detail drawn with pigment pen.

"This is more a painting that happens to be on a quilted textile surface"

Black and White Feathers, a wholecloth quilt.
139 x 168cm (54.5 x 66.5in).

Black and White Feathers, detail of dark wing.

Circe's Spell *(Linda)*

This quilt features the sorceress Circe as she pours her poisonous potion into the water at her feet. Homeric legend has it that she intended to poison her rival in love and turn her into a sea monster! My younger daughter, Frances, holding a large glass fruit bowl, adopted the pose that John William Waterhouse had created in his famous painting 'Circe Invidiosa'. I worked from the resulting photographs to sketch the face, torso and hands faintly in pencil on to a length of white cotton fabric. For the painted elements of the quilt, I used artists' quality acrylic paints mixed with fabric medium and a little water to assist the flow of colour.

I wanted a dark, moody background to surround my central figure and chose to use a piece of cotton sateen, hand-dyed by Heide Stoll-Weber. It wouldn't have been possible to achieve pale flesh tones using paint over such deep colours of dye, so the painted figure was placed on top of the background fabric, straight-stitched in place and the excess white fabric cut away close to the edge of the stitching. The charcoal grey skirt was reverse appliquéd and the long, pieced pennants inserted into the seam at the waist.

The borders were decorated with digitally embroidered lettering worked in shiny rayon threads. These were made separately before attaching them to the main body of the quilt. Heads of allium flowers were also included as a decorative feature in the borders as, according to my research, this was the herb said to protect anyone who ate it and to render Circe's spells ineffective. The head of the flower has been used as a mark of punctuation in the decorative text embroidered on the border of this quilt. Most people who saw this quilt detail would probably be completely unaware of the hidden meaning of the allium, but it gives me great personal satisfaction to know it is included for a reason other than being pretty!

Some of the swirling birds were stencilled using freezer paper masks and Markal Paintstiks and others were fabric shapes applied by bonding with a double-sided fusible web. The bird in this detail was discharged and Markal applied after quilting.

Following machine quilting, more acrylic paint was applied to the face and hair.

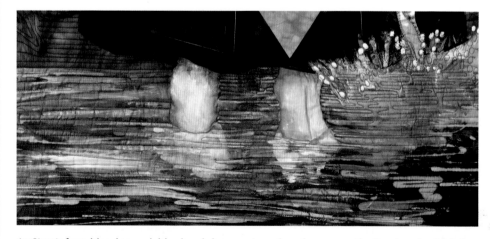

At Circe's feet, bleach was dabbed and drawn using a laundry pen on the Procion-dyed fabric. This lower section of the quilt top was immersed in clean water to stop the action of the bleach and to completely rinse it from the fabric. When it was dry, fabric paints were applied to reintroduce colour back into parts of the now pale, bleached areas.

Circe's Spell. 136 x 257cm (53.5 x 101in).

Circe pours her potion into the water and casts her magic spell

Conclusion

The quilts we both make are the result of a combination of many simple processes. The materials we use and the media we apply to them are usually quite basic and the techniques in themselves are very straightforward. If the quilts are successful, it is because we persist in layering the techniques until we achieve the results we strive for. Sometimes this is achieved quickly, involving only one or two processes. Other times a quilt will need multiple applications of a range of products and techniques. It is the initial concept leading to the design that has the most influence on the finished appearance of any of our quilts. We always know how we want something to look long before we think about ways of achieving that. We hope our book has provided an insight into our working methods and will help you to find your own approach to quiltmaking.

Suppliers

United States of America

Dharma Trading
www.dharmatrading.com
1604 Fourth Street
San Raphael
California
Extensive catalogue includes: Bleach Stop; Procion dyes and auxiliary products; fabrics for dyeing; fabric paints; fabric marker pens; safety equipment.

Jacquard Products
www.jacquardproducts.com
Rupert, Gibbon and Spider
P O Box 425
Healdsburg
CA 95448
Extensive product range includes: Discharge paste; ink-jet prepared fabrics; fabric paints.

PRO Chemical & Dye
www.prochemical.com
PO Box 14
Somerset
MA 02726
Extensive catalogue includes: Procion dyes and auxiliary products; Anti Clor; Bubble Jet Set 2000; PFD fabrics; fabric paints; fabric marker pens; plastic bottles; spray bottles; safety equipment.

United Kingdom

Ario
www.ario.co.uk
Unit 9
Garngoch Workshops
Phoenix Way
Gorseinon
Swansea
Fabric paints; Procion MX dyes; Markal Paintstiks; concentrated inks.

Art Van Go
www.artvango.co.uk
The Studios
1, Stevenage Road
Knebworth
SG3 6AN
Extensive catalogue includes: Procion dyes and auxiliary products; artists' paints and sketchbooks; papers and collage materials; compressed craft sponge; transfer foil and glue; colour shaper tools; Bubble Jet Set 2000; plastic bottles; spray bottles; safety equipment.

Crafty Computer Paper Ltd
www.craftycomputerpaper.co.uk
Swinburne Mill
Great Swinburne
Hexham
Northumberland
NE48 4DQ
Catalogue includes: heat transfer paper; fabrics treated for ink-jet printing.

Jacksons Art Supplies
www.jacksonart.co.uk
Acrylic paints; fabric paints; basic art tools and equipment; sketchbooks and papers.

Kemtex Educational Supplies
www.kemtex.co.uk
Chorley Business and Technology Centre
Euxton Lane
Chorley
Lancs PR7 6TE
Procion MX dyes and auxiliary products; information sheets.

PC World
www.pcworld.co.uk
Heat transfer paper.

Rainbow Silks
www.rainbowsilks.co.uk
85 High Street
Great Missenden
Bucks
Art media; papers and collage materials; Procion MX dyes and auxiliary products; fabrics; fabric paints; fabric marker pens; Markal Paintstiks; safety equipment.

Whaleys
www.whaleys-bradford.ltd.uk
PFD Fabrics

Canada

Opulence silks and dyes
www.opulencesilksanddyes.com
1248, Loxbury Road
North Vancouver
British Columbia
Canada V7G 1X7
Procion dyes and auxiliary products; fabric paints; fabric markers; PFD fabrics

Germany

www.patchworkshop.de
85649 Otterloh
Hauptstr 7a
Deutschland
Procion MX dyes and auxiliary products; fabrics; Markal Paintstiks.

Australia

The Thread Studio
www.thethreadstudio.com
Fabric paints and dyes; Clorox bleach pens; Bubble Jet Set 2000; Shiva Paintstiks; fabric pastels; oil pastels.

VSM (UK) Ltd
www.husqvarnaviking.com
www.pfaff.com

Robison-Anton Textile Company
175, Bergen Boulevard
Fairview
NJ 07022
USA
Machine embroidery and quilting threads.

About the authors

Linda and Laura Kemshall are renowned for their innovative approach to textiles, and their online teaching courses. They have exhibited at many prestigious events in the US and Europe to critical acclaim, and their quilts can be found in private collections worldwide. Winners of several major awards for their innovative design, use of colour and machine appliqué and quilting, Linda and Laura's international reputation continues to grow. Visit their website at www.lindakemshall.com

Acknowledgments

We are both really grateful for the advice and support of the team at the Husqvarna Viking sewing machine company (www.husqvarnaviking.com). We would also like to acknowledge the generous help we received from the Robison-Anton Textile Company (www.robison-anton.com).

Index